More Than
a Band of Metal

Loveletters From Those Who Care

Letters and photos remembering our Prisoners of War and Missing in Action. Three decades after the Vietnam War ended, questions still remain; families still search for answers and strangers have a heartfelt message to share.

Compiled and edited by the
P.O.W. NETWORK

Cover Design by: Divine & Associates, LLC, Ozark, Missouri
www.divinecentral.us

Dedication page: Original oil painting by Drew Cottril
Lithograph copyright P.O.W. NETWORK 2000

P.O.W. NETWORK
Box 68
Skidmore, MO 64487-0068

660-928-3304

or email info@pownetwork.org

Visit our website at www.pownetwork.org

IBSN 0-9723585-0-1

FORWARD

I Remember When …

As a kid growing up in the fifties I remember my Grandpa sitting me on his knee proudly sharing patriotic memories of his time in the Army. At times his eyes would fill with tears as thoughts turned to vivid memories of his buddies lost in battle. I remember other times when his aging eyes seemed to appear lost somewhere in the Argon Forrest, or in the trenches of the European Theatre. I remember too, his final days on earth when his nightmares would flare and plunge him back in time to his days of youth, days when the horrors of war carved unbelievable scars in his heart.

Now, decades since he passed away, his recollections of serving our nation still ring loud in my ears. His generation was called to, in my opinion, literally save the world. They came home to a heroes welcome and they were called "the greatest generation." My generation was asked to fight in a war the political world would not allow us to win, and when our "Johnnies" came marching home many were spit upon as they walked down the streets of America.

And so with the wisdom of 20/20 hindsight we realize the men and women who answered the call to arms during this turbulent time are every bit the heroes our fathers were in *their* time. Thousands gave their lives to fight the communist evil; thousands more were broken and scared by the horrors of battle. But there is an elite group of patriots whom I regard as the greatest-of-the-great--the men who will never be forgotten nor will their smiling faces or their passionate belief in God, family and Country. The true American heroes are the men whose names are engraved on those precious bands of metal.

I remember the first time I saw the bracelet, the name engraved wasn't a stranger, he was someone's Dad, brother, or son. Young people wore them with pride, it was *their* statement of patriotism in a time when "the elitist" bunch distained our servicemen and women. Many told me their nights were filled with prayer that "*their*" name would come home safely. In reflection they were ALL our brothers and most of us who put on a uniform have said, "But by the grace of God, go I." May God Bless them all.

Mike Radford
Ambassador of Patriotism

DEDICATION

For those that served
　　　Are serving
　　　　　And still serve

That we can live free.

CONTENTS

INTRODUCTION

With more than 90,000 men still unaccounted for since WWI, the United States had no computerized research source related totally to Prisoner of War information. Families, veterans and researchers had to rely on manual search and retrieval of paper records from hundreds of warehouses or archive offices.

The P.O.W. NETWORK was founded on Veterans Day, 1989. An educational not-for-profit 501 (c)(3), the NETWORK has spent more than 12 years electronically archiving documentation and stories on the tragedies, losses, triumphs and memories of those servicemen held captive or missing in SE Asia.

Over the years, NETWORK Chairman and founding member, Chuck Schantag, his wife Mary and the board of directors have personally met hundreds of returnees. They have recorded numerous first hand accounts of captivity experiences. In addition, they have been able to help families request copies of government records, meet those that served with their loved ones, or allow children to "know" they fathers they never grew up with. Much of the material, including the 3700+ Vietnam POW/MIA biographies, are posted for all to use on the internet. The website (www.pownetwork.org) is one of the largest of its kind in the world – housing more than 5000 online pages of documentation – maintained daily with news, changes, corrections and letter postings. Offline, thousands more documents are archived for research.

The NETWORK receives an average of 24,000 email inquiries a year, with the research returning 9000 customized lists, documents, or data files by email. The NETWORK also serves as a clearing house for mail to returnees - letters, bracelets, and queries pour in every week. The mail is forwarded to the returnee, or in rare instances, the loved one of a POW/MIA. *MOST families of those still missing cannot be directly contacted. That has resulted in an area on the NETWORK website called LOVELETTERS, where individuals can leave a public letter for the family. Those LOVELETTERS are the basis for this book.*

Each letter is accompanied, in this book, with statistical details on the POW or MIA in question. Please realize those statistics - Rank, Home of Record, etc - are as they were at TIME OF LOSS. They do not reflect current residence, promotions during captivity nor rank at retirement. The "rest of" each biography can be found on the website.

The success of our work can be measured by the families of those POW/MIAs we help. The thanks is overwhelming sometimes. The opportunity to meet our Vietnam returnees, or friends that flew with many of our missing makes all the effort worthwhile.

The explosion of Internet technology allows us to pursue more accurate histories and continuously gather information. More updates have been done on the biographies in just the last few years than in all the previous decades. We will continue to update until there is no information to be found. We're glad we can help answer the questions after 30+ years.

Please feel free to share corrections, family contacts, or any other information you might have on our POW/MIAs.

For those of you just now going to the jewel boxes, or searching for the name you knew so long ago - the information on these heroes can be found at www.pownetwork.org. If you don't have access to the internet, please write for a copy of their biography and current status.

Together, we can STILL make a difference.

Semper Fi

About the Editors:

Chuck Schantag is a Vietnam Veteran, having served in the Marine Corps with India 3/5 until being wounded on January 31, 1968 (TET). He and his wife Mary, manage the day to day activities, website updates, and research for the NETWORK. Chuck's father was a career Marine, serving in Saipan and the Mariana Islands during WWII. Mary's father served as a cook in Persia during WWII.

This book was born on the 4th of July, 2002 – remembering "with Freedom, and justice for all."

ACKNOWLEDGEMENTS

We would be remiss if we did not thank many that have helped us along the way to do what we do:

Homecoming II, Ted Sampley and Margaret Nevin for turning over the biography project to us for completion more than a decade ago.

Col. Ted Guy, for his guidance, his beliefs and the integrity that never wavered.

NAM POWs, Inc. and Capt. Mike McGrath for opening the organization, their memories and their friendships to us so we could "get it right" as we wrote their biographies.

Lynn O'Shea, The National Alliance of Families and the families of our POWs and MIAs for their trust. Also for sharing their most intimate grief, and opening their hearts in their most trying times.

Heart of Illinois POW/MIA Association for their ever-present support.

Ambassador Mike Radford, a dear friend, who kept talking till we listened and put the book together. Shari Radford for keeping the coffee fresh and the door always open.

Richard Rezac, Sandy Strait, Hank and Erika Holzer, for professional advise and support.

For our board members, advisory board, donors, BBS and website friends who have made our work meaningful, useful and historically accurate – and for those that continue to use our work, our archives, our website… Thank you.

Chapter 1

The P.O.W. Bracelet*

A simple metal band engraved with the name of a POW or MIA and the date he was lost.

Don't wear it unless you want to get involved. When one assumes the one-to-one bond with a stranger who is unable even to ask for your concern, and to enter the pain of his family, something happens to you.

You are taught new lessons about old concepts. Unity. Caring. Brotherhood.

The bracelet is worn with the vow that it will not be removed until the day that his real status is determined or that he returns home.

The bracelet is distributed by VIVA, a non-profit, non-political volunteer student organization, maintained solely by individual contribution. Donations are used to print and distribute the necessary material throughout the nation to alert all Americans to the tragic plight of the POW/MIA.

PLACE A STAR ON YOUR BRACELET

Blue and white stars are available at most POW/MIA offices or from VIVA. A blue star is placed on your bracelet if your man is still MIA. A white star is used if he is already on the list of returning POWs.

* From original marketing material by VIVA

Hoa Lo Prison, nicknamed the Hanoi Hilton by American pilots held captive there.

The idea for the bracelets was started by two fellow college students, Carol Bates and Kay Hunter, as a way to remember American prisoners of war suffering in captivity in Southeast Asia. In late 1969 television personality Bob Dornan (who several years later was elected to the US Congress) introduced the two young women and several other members of VIVA to three wives of missing pilots.

VIVA (Voices in Vital America) was started in Los Angeles as a conservative college campus organization to counteract the anti-war sentiment that was building on campuses throughout the country. The MIA wives thought the student group could assist them in drawing public attention to the prisoners and missing in Vietnam. The idea of circulating petitions and letters to Hanoi demanding humane treatment for the POWs was appealing, as they were looking for ways college students could become involved in positive programs to support US soldiers without becoming embroiled in the controversy of the war itself.

Ideas to bring the plight of our POWs/MIAs before the American people were being discussed at a meeting with the above mentioned people and we decided on the idea of a bracelet similar to Bob Dornan's, Montagnard bracelet. After returning from Vietnam, Dornan , a former USAF fighter pilot vowed that he would not remove the bracelet until the war in Vietnam ended and the POWs he knew were home.

He was associated at that time with Gloria Coppin, (wife of the L.A. industrialist, Doulas Coppin) Carol Bates and Steve Frank of Voices In Vital America (VIVA). A discussion ensued, with the resulting idea that each bracelet be inscribed with the name of a different POW or MIA with the wearer promising to wear the bracelet of his of her POW/MIA until he either came home or his fate was known.

The major problem was that VIVA had no money to make bracelets, although their advisor was able to find a small shop in Santa Monica that did engraving on silver used to decorate horses. The owner agreed to make 10 sample bracelets. The committee sat around in Coppin's kitchen with the engraver on the telephone, as they tried to figure out what would put on the bracelets. That is why they engraved only name, rank and date of loss, since, in the rush, they didn't have time to think of anything else.

Armed with the sample bracelets, VIVA set out to find someone who would donate money to make bracelets for distribution to college students. It had not yet occurred to them that adults would want to wear the things, as they weren't very attractive. Outright funding and loans could not be secured. Finally in the late summer of 1970, Gloria Coppin's husband donated enough brass and copper to make 1,200 bracelets. The Santa Monica engraver agreed to make them and except payment at a later date from any proceeds they might realize.

The first four bracelets made and circulated were:
John K. Hardy, USAF MIA
Arthur Mearns, USAF MIA
Roosevelt Hestle, USAF MIA and
Stephen P. Hanson, USMC MIA.

The concept of the bracelet was introduced at a VIVA banquet in Beverly Hills with the wives of the four men above in attendance. It was VIVA's policy that a man's name was not used unless permission was granted by the family.

Although the initial bracelets were going to cost about 75 cents to make, VIVA was unsure about how much they should ask people to donate to receive a bracelet. In 1970, a student admission to the local movie theater was $2.50. They decided this seemed like a fair price to ask from a student for one of the nickel-plated bracelets. They also made copper ones for adults who believed they helped their "tennis elbow." Again, according to the logic, adults could pay more, so they requested $3.00 for the copper bracelets.

At the suggestion of local POW/MIA relatives, VIVA attended the National League of Families annual meeting in Washington, DC in late September. They were amazed at the interest of the wives and parents in having their man's name put on bracelets and in obtaining them for distribution. Bob Dornan, who was always a champion of the POW/MIAs and their families, continued to publicize the issue on his Los Angeles television talk show and promoted the bracelets.

Carol Hanson became the National Chairman of the POW/MIA Bracelet Campaign. Entertainers Bob Hope and Martha Raye served as honorary co-chairmen.

On Veterans Day, November 11, 1970, VIVA officially kicked off the bracelet program with a news conference at the Universal Sheraton Hotel. Public response quickly grew and they eventually got to the point were they were receiving over 12,000 requests a day. This also brought money in to pay whatever else they could do to publicize the POW/MIA issue. They formed a close alliance with the relatives of missing men. VIVA also tried to furnish these groups with all the stickers and other literature they could give away.

As time went on and the bracelets became more and more popular, other family groups began to make bracelets and thus you see some that are a little different than the original bracelet. The stars were added later. The blue star denoting MIA and the white star denoting a POW.

Many prominent individuals from all walks of life (Richard Nixon, General William Westmoreland, Johnny Cash, Charlton Heston, Sonny and Cher, Bob Hope) did wear the bracelet. The program was supported by schools, junior chambers of commerce, airline pilots and the public in general. The bracelet wearer, identifying with one individual, became much more personally involved with the whole POW/MIA issue and it is believed the bracelets helped greatly in solidifying the concern of the American people for all our POWs and MIAs."

VIVA alone distributed nearly five million bracelets and raised enough money to produce untold millions of bumper stickers, buttons, brochures, matchbooks, newspaper ads, etc., to draw attention to the missing men. In 1976, VIVA closed its doors forever.

Sadly, it was NOT the end of the POW/MIA issue. There were still unanswered questions and waiting families. Bracelets are now made by engravers nationwide and are *still* worn by millions of caring individuals.

Our thanks to Carol Bates Brown, Carole Hansen Hickerson and
Capt Duffy Hutton, USN (Ret) for information used in this chapter.

Members of the Joint Command

Negotiations

Chapter 2

In Recognition

Every year, by proclamation, the President of the United States declares April 9th as "National Former Prisoner of War Recognition Day." This date honors those that CAME HOME from any war. In the past decade, an average of TWELVE returnees (all wars) have died EACH DAY.

National POW/MIA Recognition Day is by law, the 3rd Friday in September every year. This date honors those men and women still held in enemy hands or buried on foreign soil.

On August 10, 1990, the Congress passed a bill recognizing the black and white, POW/MIA flag as "the symbol of our Nation's concern and commitment to resolving as fully as possible the fate of Americans still prisoner, missing and unaccounted for in Southeast Asia..."

In 1997, bills passed the House and Senate mandating the POW/MIA flag be flown on specific holidays. The 1998 Defense Authorization act noted that the flag MUST be flown on: Memorial Day, Armed Forces Day, Flag Day, Veterans Day, Independence Day, POW/MIA Recognition Day.

In 1998, the Veterans Administration noted the flag _will_ fly EVERY day at their facilities.

In front, Zuhoski, Cmd. Charles P., USN (Ret) and Copeland, Col. H.C., USAF (Ret)
Right side, 3rd row, Wilson, Maj. Hal III, USAF (Ret). Photos taken 03/14/73.

Butler, Capt. William, USAF (Ret)

Chapter 3

Statistics

ALL POW/MIAs are now noted as PFOD*
except Gulf War MIA Michael Speicher

WWI	116,708	KIA
	204,002	Wounded
	3,350	POW/MIA [pfod]
WWII	407, 316	KIA
	670,846	Wounded
	78,777	POW/MIA [pfod]
Korea	54,246	KIA
	153, 303	Wounded
	7,190	POWs [4,428 repatriated); 8177 MIAs [pfod]
Vietnam	58,151	KIA
	303, 678	Wounded
	2,459	POW/MIA [pfod] 1973
	1907	Still "Unaccounted for" as of Aug 05, 2002**
Gulf War**	382	KIA
	467	Wounded
	37	KIA/BNR or non battle BNR***
	3	MIA +
	1,947	KIA OUTSIDE Combat theater

*PFOD,   "Presumptive Finding of Death" Mandated court hearing per Missing Service Personnel Act   ** Department of Defense, Washington Headquarters Services, Directorate for Information Operations and Reports *** BNR – Body Not Recovered. + The number 3 was used by President George Bush in the September 20, 2002 POW/MIA Recognition Day Proclamation.

Chapter 4

The Category Definitions
(as used by the United States Government during the Vietnam War)

Categories of Degrees of Information
Enemy knowledge of POW/MIA

Category 1, Confirmed knowledge
A. Identified by the enemy by name
B. Identified by reliable sources. Received from releasee/escapee
or
C. Reported by highly reliable intelligence sources
D. Identified through analysis of all -source intelligence.

Category 2, Suspect knowledge
A. Involved in the same incidents as individuals in Category 1.
B. Lost in areas or under conditions that they may reasonably be expected to be known by the enemy.
C. Connected with an incident that was discussed but not identified by name in the enemy news media, or
D. Probably identified through analysis of all-source intelligence.

Category 3, Doubtful knowledge
This category contains individuals whose loss incident such that it is doubtful that the enemy would have knowledge of the specific individuals. (e.g., aircrews lost over water or remote areas.)

Category 4, Unknown Knowledge
A. Individuals whose time and place of incident are unknown (e.g., aircrews members downed at the unknown locations or ground personnel that were separated from their units at an unknown time or place), and
B. Who do not meet criteria of categories 1 through 3.

Category 5, Category unrelated to degree of enemy knowledge.
A. Individuals whose remains have been determined to be non-recoverable as outlined in Department of the Army Technical Manual 10-286, January 1964, section 39.

Data from Defense Intelligence Agency -- January 20, 1982

Gia Lam airfield near Hanoi

Chapter 5

From an M.I.A. Daughter

FATHER: MOORE, THOMAS

Rank/Branch: E6/U.S. Air Force
Date of Birth: 09 December 1929
Home City of Record: Baton Rouge LA
Date of Loss: 31 October 1965
Country of Loss: South Vietnam
Status in 1973: Prisoner of War
Category: 1
Acft/Vehicle/Ground: Ford Truck
Other Personnel in Incident: Charles Dusing; Samuel Adams (both POW), Jasper Page, escapee.

DAUGHTER: Nora Diane Moore
Friday, May 10, 2002

I wrote this last night, it came all of a sudden and I wanted to share it.

I am the daughter of a forgotten HERO. I am the daughter of an Airman who gave his life and his freedom for me.

In the most feeble attempts of writing this I can only hope that when someone reads it that they attempt to understand my feelings, I can not write for my sisters, I can not write for the other children of war, I can however bring to the fore front the differences between Killed in Action and Missing in Action.

There are many Americans who do not have the littlest idea of what it is like to try to comprehend what war does to children, from the smallest toddler to the oldest child who tries to understand why my daddy went away. I have wonderful friends who know what it is like to loose a parent, many whose parent was lost to heart attacks, car crashes, and suicides. These friends and I acknowledge each other's lost and understand the loneliness of being without mom or dad. However there are only a few of us who understand those loses coming from war. We all share in the same questions, the same heartaches, and the same wishes. The biggest shared question being the "What If".

I have read so many stories from the Children of the Wall, Children of the Vietnam War dead. The ones whose names are forever carved into black granite. Well over 58,000 names of men and women, who stand vigil night and day to remind those who pass in front of them That Freedom has a price, and that price is not money, but blood of fellow Americans.

Reading stories from Vets, history and other materials is what has educated us to believe many things about Vietnam. Some good and some bad. Movies have done the same.

I was a young girl of 11 when my dad went into his Missing in Action status. Later it was confirmed that enemy forces while returning to base after a 24-hour pass had captured him and three of his friends.

My dad and the others in the wrong place at the wrong time. No way to defend themselves, nor did they have the chance.

A simple return to base that ended up a terrifying event.

Years have gone by, which in turn have turned in to decades. My sisters and I have families of our own, and my father has grandchildren and a great grand son. Yet there is still the man who is Missing.

I remember like other children of our time the Yellow Cab delivering the telegram, the one that makes mom cry out a very heart-breaking sob.

I remember like others those words, We regret to Inform you...

And the other words depending on the status were either, your husband has been Killed in Action or is Missing in Action.

This is where my story will differ from other Sons and Daughters of the Vietnam war, except for a small number. As you see there are less that 2,000 men still listed now has Missing in Action. So that means we MIA kids are very few, the forgotten ones.

When my dad went Missing I remember asking the big question of my 11 years. What do you mean my daddy is missing, and why can't they find him. How do you lose a grown up man. This followed me all my life, even after growing up, it is hard to understand why my dad and the other MIA's cannot be accounted for. And it is really hard to understand if it is the men who were last seen alive.

Year after Year, the haunting realization comes, daddy is not coming home.

Yet there is no body to bury, there is no funeral, there is not a grave to visit, there is nothing. NO closure.

We were and are still expected to take the harsh reality of our dads Missing in Action and to get on with our life's. And WE DID. With little of no help from any one but our moms and each other, but the each other only came after we were grown.

Our country was torn apart by Vietnam, our flag was burned by Americans, men and women protested our presence in South East Asia, some dodged the draft, and those who went to served were spat upon when they returned,. They were called baby killers, and no one wanted any thing to do with them, no ticker tape parades no welcome homes.

Coffins with flags draped on them returned to American soil and the children grieved, and said good-bye to daddy.

Yet those whose bodies did not come home were never thought about except by the families and friends. There were those who were Killed in Action bodies not recovered or returned but evidence to the fact that they indeed were killed. Those families are like us MIA families. They have that same haunting feeling, could my dad still be really alive.

Telegrams came, in the thousands, widows were made, and children grew up to fast.

My mom got hers, and I grew up, the oldest of three girls is not easy. My Christmas's turned into learning how to put toys together, and wrap gifts that Santa is supposed to do.

I even learned how to change fuses at 11, and by the time I was 14, I could change the oil in the car.

Yet I was protected somewhat by my mom, she did a great job raising my sisters and me, the best she could do. Yet she could not stop those who told me my dad was also a baby killer, who spat on my sisters, and me or who told me my dad deserved everything he got.

That is hard to understand when you are a little girl, still hard for me to understand now.

Plus mom told us to not talk about dads case, as she said it might not be good for those men who are POW's and if daddy is a POW we don't want to jeopardize his coming home.

Neither was it a good idea to talk with men who had been over there because we don't what to upset them. Whether or not those men were uncles or even cousins.

Now years later we have talked with the men who served and came home , we learned about our dads, and we learned about Vietnam. The men were just as glad to talk as we were to listen.

Yet there is still a difference in the MIA kid, we talk to the Vets, we listen to them, we ask them questions and they help a lot.

We share our stories with others , but our dad's stories are as some would like to say still to political. So not to many people will ask us to speak at functions, yet we still hear, get over it.

We truly have no real place in the Vietnam organizations out there, and don't get me wrong, there are a few that we belong to. Yet I can truthfully say there is fewer that really recognizes who we are. There are those who say that they are working towards the POW MIA issue, but only use it to benefit them when it is needed.

No one knows what it is like to live year after year wondering where is my dad but the MIA child, no one can even come near telling me they understand unless it is another MIA kid.

No one but the MIA child or family member knows what the Missing Man Formation means unless you lost your dad to a plane crash some where and his remains were never found, or a small hand full of broken fragments comes decades later. No on but the MIA child or family member understands the Table Ceremony for the POW MIA, no one but the loved one who sits in silence with a tear as the meaning is read.

To feel happiness and jealously at the same time is another feeling that is something we deal with, happiness when another MIA is found, recovered, and returned to his home land and to his children and loved one, jealousy when you want so much to be standing the same way,

Watching a flag draped coffin being so gently carried to a final resting place ,wishing it was your turn to say good-bye.

To my fellow MIA sisters and Brothers, we are very special, we are children who have kept the eternal flame alive that our dads gave us when he became our dad.

Our dads may have been forgotten, by the general population, and we may but a few, but we have a voice and we have the time to make sure we continue the legacy our moms put before us.

As this Memorial Day approaches we all need to remember.

Never Forget.
Diane Moore
Proud Daughter of
CMSGT THOMAS MOORE-USAF
POW-MIA unaccounted for
October 31 1965

Moore, Thomas – POW/DIC/PFOD, top
Shelton Charles – POW/PFOD, bottom left; Humphrey, Galen – KIA/BNR, bottom right

Chapter 6

Strangers Have a Message

LYON, JAMES MICHAEL
Rank/Branch: O3/U.S. Army
Unit: HHC, 2nd Brigade, 101st Airborne Division
Date of Birth: 08 March 1948
Home City of Record: Indianapolis IN
Date of Loss: 05 February 1970
Country of Loss: South Vietnam
Status (in 1973): Prisoner of War
Category: 2
Aircraft/Vehicle/Ground: UH1H
Other Personnel in Incident: Tom Y. Kobashigawa, John W. Parsels, Daniel H. Hefel (returned POWs)
REMARKS: 700206 Died In Captivity

From: Debi Nemnich
Thu, 15 Jan 1998

CAPT. JAMES LYON - my hero, my unknown friend

As a senior in high school, some 30 years ago, I purchased a POW/MIA bracelet and placed it upon my wrist. Today it is still there bearing the name of CAPT. JAMES LYON (2-5-70). It stares up at me as a reminder of the tragedy of war and the failure of our government to take extraordinary means to bring our men home. Although I do not know Capt. Lyon or his family, when I went to Washington, DC for the sole purpose of seeing 'The Wall', I broke down in tears simply by finding his name in the book. The book is too big, the wall contains too many names. My heart goes out to all the men and their families. What a sacrifice to maintain the freedom we all enjoy. I thank God that my father was a veteran and bestowed upon me a patriotism I wish our young people would come to practice.

To read the letters contained in this page and knowing that there are too many bracelets out there makes me want to shake some sense into our countries leaders and cry out to them to help bring Capt. Lyon home along with all the others and bring these families the peace they haven't had in far too many years. I have not only come to love Capt. Lyon, but the countless others, the heroes that have returned and all soldiers willing to conquer the foe. If Capt. Lyon has any family member reading this, please know that I have come to love his man I did not have the pleasure of knowing. For 30+ years his bracelet has been gracing my wrist. It is a source of pride for me the share with others what it means and why it remains on my arm. My husband told me years ago it was time to remove it - the war was over. The war may be over, but I have not yet been informed that Capt. Lyon is home, so it stays right where it is!!

May God bless all of you! You are in my heart and in my prayers.

Debi

Family and friends met every plane as they touched down at airbases across the U.S.

From: "Kelley, Michael S. CW3
Date: Fri, 21 Sep 2001 13:35:22 -0500
POW/MIA Recognition Day

Ladies and Gentlemen,

I would like to take this opportunity to thank you and your comrades for the sacrifices you have so gallantly made for our country. I know the events of the past few days have overwhelmed us all, however, I wish to re-assure you that they have in no way diminished, rather intensified the meaning behind your sacrifices. Thank You far everything,

Very Respectfully,

Michael S. Kelley
CW3, USA
Brigade Tactical Operations Officer
159th Aviation Brigade

Returnee Unknown

MORRISSEY, ROBERT DAVID
Rank/Branch: O4/U.S. Air Force
Unit: 474th Tactical Fighter Wing, Takhli AB, Thailand
Date of Birth: 24 April 1930
Home City of Record: Albuquerque NM
Date of Loss: 07 November 1972
Country of Loss: Laos
Status (in 1973): Missing In Action
Category: 4
Acft/Vehicle/Ground: F111A
Other Personnel In Incident: Robert Mack Brown (missing)

From: Heather Sterne
7 Nov 1999

November 7th...
Another year has come and gone and there is no new information about LTC Robert D Morrissey. Today marks the 27th anniversary of his disappearance after his plane was downed over Laos in 1972.

I chose a POW-MIA bracelet with LTC Morrissey's name on it because we are both from the state of New Mexico and his disappearance coincides with my brother's birthday (to the year!). How could I ever forget! I haven't, and I was just checking this site for any new developments. Hopefully next year...

In the meantime, my best wishes to LTC Morrissey's family and friends.

Sincerely,

Heather S.

PLASSMEYER, BERNARD HERBERT
Rank/Branch: O2/U.S. Marine Corps
Unit: Marine Attack Squadron 311
Date of Birth: 05 May 1945
Home City of Record: Freeburg MO
Date of Loss: 11 September 1970
Country of Loss: South Vietnam
Status (in 1973): Missing In Action
Category: 2
Acft/Vehicle/Ground: A4E

From: Donna Jean Slaughter
01 Oct 2001

To the family of Lt. Bernard H. Plassmeyer,

This is being sent to you in the hope that it will bring you a little comfort. My name is Donna and I have a POW/MIA bracelet with Bernard's name on it. This is my second one, as the original had broken and needed to be replaced. You are not alone, and I HAVE NOT FORGOTTEN & NEVER WILL. My heart goes out to you, his son, wife, parents and relatives.

September 11 now has two meanings for me...

One is the Attack on the World Trade Center and the other is the day Bernard's plane went down-9-11-70.

God bless you and keep you always, and may God bless America.

Donna

From: Cori Batte-Lynch
11 Nov 1999

Thank you! on Veteran's Day

I sit at my desk today and think of the cookies I baked and packed carefully in coffee cans, the paperback books I collected from neighbors, and the silly fifth-grade letters written to brave young men in the jungle, some incarcerated by the enemy, some awaiting disability or death. I want to thank all those who contributed to the cause, no matter how un-noble some may say it was. A special thanks for those who took the time to write back to young people praying for peace, and thank you to my fifth-grade teacher (I wish I remembered her name), who made us realize that you were not just soldiers, but brothers, fathers and sons. And lastly, thanks to God and my grandfather's genetics that gave my big brother flat feet, so the draft rejected him. I remember and honor you.

Cori

Hess, Lt. Col Jay, USAF (Ret)

CALLOWAY, PORTER EARL

Rank/Branch: E5/U.S. Army
Unit: Company B, 3rd Battalion, 21st Infantry, 196th Light
Infantry Brigade
Date of Birth: 16 January 1947 (Lillie LA)
Home City of Record: Bernice LA
Date of Loss: 11 March 1968
Country of Loss: South Vietnam
Status (in 1973): Missing In Action
Category: 2
Aircraft/Vehicle/Ground: Ground

From: Ali Leone
31 Oct 2001

Hello there. My name is Ali Leone, and I served in the Army for four years, during that time, I learned a lot about POWS/MIAS from my father. My father also served in Vietnam, and like so many, he lost a lot of friends. I met a sergeant in the military one day who was wearing a bracelet with a man's name on it. I assumed it was a relative, but he told me the story behind his bracelet and what it stood for. I thought it was a small, quiet but wonderful show of support for those who suffered and gave their lives for their country. Somehow though, it still did not seem real to me -- war, I mean, and all that it entails. To me, the military was an opportunity to better my life. Recently, I mentioned this to a friend and told him that I wished I could do more than just wear a bracelet -- that somehow that didn't seem enough. He told me that anything we could do to show our support to these service members and their families was enough -- no matter how large or small. Today, I got my bracelet. It bears the name of SSgt. Porter Calloway. I logged on the internet tonight to see if I could learn more about SSgt. Calloway. What I found was a devastatingly long list of service members' names. It tore at my heart to see so many - for the first time, I have realized the true devastation of war. I don't know that SSgt. Calloway's family will ever read this, but I want them to know that where ever I go from now until I die, he will be with me. I did not know this man, but I love him. I love him for his willingness to serve his country, to make the world a better place for us all. It is him, and so other many like him, that make this country great.

Without ever having met him, his story, his courage and his service to his country has forever changed my life.

So, to his family I say, don't ever think he will be forgotten by others. His service to his country did not go unnoticed. I will take his legacy with me everywhere, and know that he is a symbol of what my service commitment was really all about -- not bettering my future job opportunities, but a chance to make a better life for everyone, to represent my country and what it stands for. I always have felt a great pride in my country, and more so when I served, but now I truly understand the depth and the meaning of being a United States Soldier. I hope to one day meet you, and more so be able to give you this small token of my support.

Thank you for creating a hero, a teacher -- a soldier.

Ali

Navy returnee unknown

Lock Ninh air strip. Choppers were there for many hours before POWs were allowed to leave.

CREED, BARTON SHELDON
Rank/Branch: O3/U.S. Navy
Date of Birth: 03 April 1945
Home City of Record: Peekskill NY
Date of Loss: 13 March 1971
Country of Loss: Laos
Status (In 1973): Prisoner of War
Category: 2
Acft/Vehicle/Ground: A7E

From: Diane L Moseley
2 Nov 2001

To Susan Page Creed Percy

My name is Diane, I live in Kingston, and I have worn the bracelet of Barton S. Creed for many years. Several years ago I found information about Barton on the internet regarding his POW status. This information stated that Barton was unmarried. To my shock today while searching again for any additional new information about Barton I came across the update that he was indeed married and had 2 children.

Please know that Barton will always be remembered in my heart and that if you would like his bracelet I am willing to part with it for your and your children other wise I will wear the bracelet that bears his name until he is brought home. I would very much like to hear from you to learn more about him and if there is anything I can do to help.

Diane

From: Susan Creed Percy
3 Nov 2001

Diane

Bart's whole family and I are so grateful to people like you who have worn Bart's bracelet for so many years. You have kept his memory alive by keeping him in your heart.

Each of us has a bracelet and some wearers have given their bracelets to Bart's children. I would encourage you to keep the one you've worn because while we have a better idea of what happened to him, he has yet to be found and brought home.

Where is Kingston? I thought perhaps New York since that is Bart's home state. Let me know your specific questions about Bart and I'll be glad to answer them.

Best,

Susan Creed Percy

BOGARD, LONNIE PAT
Rank/Branch: O3/U.S. Air Force
Unit: 435th Tactical Fighter Squadron, Ubon Thailand
Date of Birth: 11 May 1942
Home City of Record: Metairie LA
Date of Loss: 12 May 1972
Country of Loss: Laos
Status (in 1973): Missing in Action
Category: 4
Aircraft/Vehicle/Ground: F4D
Other Personnel in Incident: William H. Ostermeyer (missing)

From: Judyth M McDonald
17 Dec 1999

I am 52 years old and I have had a bracelet for almost 30 years of CAPT. LONNIE PAT BOGARD who was in the Air Force MIA May 12, 1972.

I just wanted you let you know that I lived a lot of places and have rid my self of many things in moving but I have had a special place in my heart for Lonnie Bogard; who I have never met but who I think of often. There are still people out there who still love him and pray for his safe return just like I have done.

I just wanted to let you know that someone you have never met; cares. As the years go by I wonder and care even more and I wish I could see that he is finally returned safe to those that love him. I would love nothing more than to give this bracelet to his family; that would mean he is back home like he should be.

I have not forgotten and never will.

Judyth McDonald

Terwilliger, Virgil – KIA/BNR, top left
Pool, Jerry Lynn – MIA/PFOD, group remains I.D. disputed by family, top right;
Gourley, Laurent, MIA/PFOD, bottom.

COEN, HARRY BOB
Rank/Branch: E3/U.S. Army
Unit: Company E, 2nd Battalion, 1st Infantry, 196th Infantry Brigade, 3rd
Infantry Division (Americal)
Date of Birth: 22 September 1948 (Lander WY)
Home City of Record: Riverton WY
Date of Loss: 12 May 1968
Country of Loss: South Vietnam
Status (in 1973): Missing in Action
Category: 2
Aircraft/Vehicle/Ground: Ground

From: Laurie Holbrook
20 September 1998

As I was cleaning out my desk, I came across my POW bracelet. I sat back and remembered when I got it, so long ago and how I wore it each day, checking and hoping he made it home.

I have just checked the listings and find he is still MIA, how my heart sank, tears down my face. My children looked at it and asked so many questions and I told them how proud I was to wear it and now again it graces my wrist.

His name is Harry Coen.

Laurie Holbrook

ARMISTEAD, STEVEN RAY
Rank/Branch: O2/U.S. Marine Corps
Unit: VMA 533, Marine Air Group 12
Date of Birth: 15 June 1944
Home City of Record: Los Angeles CA
Date of Loss: 17 March 1969
Country of Loss: Laos
Status (in 1973): Missing In Action
Category: 2
Aircraft/Vehicle/Ground: A6A

From: BJ Johns
22 Dec 2001

For: relatives and friends of Steven R. Armistead, Captain, USMC.

I have recently gotten very interested in Marine Corps history, as well as American War History, WW II, Korea, and Vietnam. I bought a POW bracelet and it had his name on it. I found out as much as I could about him, and when my sister and I went to Washington DC for the Marine Corps Birthday Ball and Veteran's Day, we went to the WALL and I got his name etched on paper, (now framed on my living room wall above his incident report, all next to a poster of the Flag going up on Mt Suribachi, Iwo Jima.) as well as still photos and videotape of his name on the WALL.

Captain Armistead is now considered to be part of my family, and our prayers. I may not know what he looks like, but as a fellow Marine, he's my older brother. I have recently introduced my family to the POW/MIA family, and I hope they embrace it as I have.

To those who have served before me, thank you. For those who have gone Home, but not to this home on earth, I'll see you someday. Thank you my brothers.

Robert Johns Jr, Lcpl, USMC

ELLIOT, ROBERT MALCOLM
Remains Returned 12/27/99

Rank/Branch: O3/U.S. Air Force
Unit: 34th Tactical Fighter Squadron, Korat Airbase, Thailand
Date of Birth: 08 November 1929
Home City of Record: Springfield MA
Date of Loss: 14 February 1968
Country of Loss: North Vietnam
Status (in 1973): Missing In Action
Category: 2
Aircraft/Vehicle/Ground: F105D

From: Chick Candler
11 Dec 2001

To the Elliot family,

I have worn/saved/shown Maj. Robert Elliot's POW/MIA bracelet for over 30 years now. I got it in high school in 1970 or early 1971,and wore it for many years. At some point, like so many others, I quit wearing it, but I never forgot it or lost track of it. Every so often I would try to find out if Maj. Elliot had returned or not. Once was in Washington D.C. at The Wall where several groups were passing out information on POW/MIA's.

Another time, a friend of mine in Atlanta had the address of a group that had information on POW/MIA's. Both of these times, as well as others, no new information had been found. Today, however, was a different matter. For some reason I was looking at his bracelet in its display case when I had the idea of using the internet to search for him. When I typed in his name in the POW/MIA search field I hesitated to hit "enter". I was apprehensive as to what I would find - to say the least! But now at last I know - after 30+ years he is home. While he did not return in the manner you, or I, or anyone would have liked, there is, at the very least, closure.

I feel a little strange about all of this being over (so to speak), but Lord only knows how you must have felt! My 4 year old daughter was with me when I found out about Maj. Elliot and wanted to know what those tears on my face were. Right then I book marked this site so we may learn together just what happened when her daddy was a lot younger. My sincerest hope is that GOD has blessed you in the intervening years. If you would like the bracelet please let me know, as I would be honored for you to have it. For now, it is in a place of honor for my family.

Sincere best wishes,

Chick Candler

Davis, Capt. Edward USN (Ret) and Ma-Co

EDGAR, ROBERT J.
Rank/Branch: O2/U.S. Air Force
Date of Birth: 21 May 1943
Home City of Record: Venice, FL
Date of Loss: 05 February 1968
Country of Loss: Laos
Status (in 1973): Missing In Action
Category: 4
Acft/Vehicle/Ground: RF-4C
Other Personnel in Incident: William T. Potter (missing)

From: Zoe Rose Treuer
12 Apr 2000

Hello,

I am a sophomore in college this year, and I'm in the Air Force ROTC program. Having hippies for parents and yet having some kind of kinship with the military, I've gotten to hear all sides of every argument concerning Vietnam. And still, I don't know too much about it. I'm 19, and have no concept of war, not really. Recently, my detachment ordered POW/MIA bracelets and I bought one. Why? I couldn't tell you ... my parents would say it's foolish, my friends would think it overly sentimental.

I'll tell you what, though: I put on this bracelet, which states the name of Captain Robert J. Edgar and his disappearance date of 5 Feb 1968, hometown FL, lost in Laos, and I've never felt stranger.

I can't take it off; the thought that this man, 25 years old when he disappeared, was doing what I shall be doing soon: fighting for my country. I cannot believe that it is unknown what happened to him, that he's not home either with his wife or resting in peace. He is out there somewhere while I am here. I have been obsessed with finding out about him, and the internet has been a wonderful asset.

I am shocked at my reaction to this bracelet! I will never take it off, I am sure of that - not until he comes home somehow, or his family requests it, of course.

If you are out there, Edgar family, I want you to know that in no way whatsoever is Robert J Edgar forgotten. Maybe I have gotten into this tradition late, but it is never to late to love, respect, and remember in any way we can, those who gave us our freedom.

I am young; and yet, I know I'll never forget.

Sincerely and respectfully,
Zoe Rose Treuer

Returnee Unknown

WHITE, JAMES BLAIR

Rank/Branch: O3/U.S. Air Force
Unit: 357th Tactical Fighter Squadron
Date of Birth: 14 March 1942
Home City of Record: St. Petersburg FL
Date of Loss: 24 November 1969
Country of Loss: Laos
Status (in 1973): Missing in Action
Category: 4
Aircraft/Vehicle/Ground: F105D

Note: James White's brother was Astronaut Edward H. White. Edward White (an AF Col.) was killed on January 27, 1967, along with Astronauts Gus Grissiom and Roger Chaffee, when a fire swept through their Apollo spacecraft during training session. Their father was a retired AF General, at the time. He lost both his children.

From: Landy Johnson
26 May 1999

I hold the MIA bracelet for Capt. James Blair White (USAF). I purchased the bracelet on March 9, 1973, and though I don't wear it often it sits on top of my jewelry box and I think about it daily. Recently a friend who is a Vietnam vet offered to get me info on Capt. White. This friend kindly presented me with a folder containing printouts from your site and others with a biography and photos. This was the first detailed information I had ever received about Capt. White, although I had been told my two men manning a card table at the Wall in 1988 that White's plane had gone down over Laos. It was actually rather overwhelming to receive all this detailed information so many years later.

I was also overwhelmed to see that he was listed as "died while missing," and I logged onto your site to see if I could find out how it was known that he is actually dead. It was a slap in the face to see that all the MIAs were declared dead! I had no idea. I had planned to return the bracelet, but in view of the purely administrative declaration I will keep the bracelet until I hear something further. Please be aware that there are many of us who are still aware of the MIA issue, though on the periphery. These men are in our daily thoughts and prayers.

Landy Johnson

BOBE, RAYMOND EDWARD

Rank/Branch: E3/U.S. Army
Unit: Headquarters Company, USARV
Date of Birth: 30 August 1948
Home City of Record: Tarrant AL
Date of Loss: 16 March 1969
Country of Loss: South Vietnam
Status (in 1973): Missing In Action
Category: 4
Acft/Vehicle/Ground: U21A

From: Kaye Johnsen
29 Dec 2001

Dear Family Members:

I received my bracelet with the name of your loved one in November of 1974 My son was very young and as he grew often asked about the bracelet with the simple inscription. I would explain as best I could. When he left home in 1996 to make his way in the world I asked if he would like to take something with him so that he would always feel connected to home. He asked for the bracelet and I gave it to him. He is now an ordained minister and served congregations of the poor and needy here and then went to Africa to minister there. He has worn that bracelet throughout the United States and the Continent of Africa. He says that people often ask about it and he explains as best he can. As we did when he was a child, he prays that Raymond (forgive us for using his first name, but he has been with us for so long) will be returned to those who love him.

I recently found that I could get another bracelet with "our Raymond's" name and have ordered it. Perhaps a new generation will ask and I will explain it as best I can.

Our love and our prayers go out to you and we will continue to pray for PFC Raymond E. Bobe until he is home.

Kaye Johnsen

DEAN, MICHAEL FRANK
Remains returned

Rank/Branch: E5/U.S. Air Force
Unit: 40th Aerospace Rescue/Recovery Squadron, Udorn Airfield, Thailand
Date of Birth: 13 September 1946
Home City of Record: LaPuente CA
Date of Loss: 30 June 1970
Country of Loss: Laos
Status (in 1973): Killed/Body Not Recovered
Category: 2
Acft/Vehicle/Ground: HH53C

Remains were returned 03/95 as "120 bone fragments which cannot be degregated, fragments too small for DNA testing as it would "destroy the chips", a dental prostheses, a St. Christopher's medal, coins, buttons, etc. They say the fragments represent a minimum of one person, a maximum of two people, yet they feel this is a full accounting of five men who served our government..."

> *FROM a letter to the Editor, Rochelle News Leader, March 30, 1995, by Dawn Wyatt, niece of Leroy C. Schaneberg.*

From: Luc Lambert
24 Sep 1998

To the Family of Michael F. Dean,

Since 1988, I have faithfully worn Michael's bracelet and I have prayed for both his return and your comfort. I chose to wear his bracelet because I was also [at that time] an Air Force Staff Sergeant. You should know that I found great strength from him, and it wasn't until my entry into Officer Training School in 1993 that I discovered he was KIA.

However, this did not change my commitment. On July 18, 1998, I attended many events honoring POW/MIA Recognition Day. It was on this day I learned Michael's remains were returned in 1995 and I was to return the bracelet to the Wall. I am somewhat embarrassed it took me so long to find out something so utterly important to you, but nevertheless, I am elated he now rests eternally on American land. Yet, I will not place the bracelet anywhere except in the possession of Michael's family.

I have always held Michael, and his ultimate sacrifice, very close to my heart. Please rest assured that he changed my life in a very positive way. I will continue to pray for him and his family.

God bless,

Luc J.F. Lambert, Captain, USAF

Thompson, Floyd Col. USA (Ret) Longest Held POW, deceased

CARPENTER, ALLAN RUSSELL

Name: Allan Russell Carpenter
Rank/Branch: O3/U.S. Navy
Unit: Attack Squadron 72, USS Franklin D. Roosevelt (CVA 42)
Date of Birth: 14 March 1938 (Portland ME)
Home City of Record: Springvale ME
Date of Loss: 01 November 1966
Country of Loss: North Vietnam
Status (in 1973): Released POW
Aircraft/Vehicle/Ground: A4E
Other Personnel in Incident: (none missing)

From: Laura Stapf
07/01/2002

I wasn't sure how to send this email to loveletters, or to have my bracelet returned to the Carpenter Family.

I was 12 years old when I received Allan Carpenters bracelet. I am now 45. I was able to write to his wife and his children for several years, until the most blessed news that he was coming home. Allan Carpenter wrote me a very nice letter back to me when he returned. I still remember that day when I received his letter. I went back directly to church, lit every candle that was available, and cried in thanking our Lord for bringing him home to his family. His bracelet now sits along my fathers Fire Department badges, and mementos, since losing his life to asbestos cancer after 35 years as a Los Angeles County Fire Department Captain. I would like to know how I can write to the family, and return the bracelet to Allan Carpenter and his family where it truly belongs. I live in Nashville, TN, which isn't too far from Virginia. My name as a young girl was Laura Stapf. My married name is Laura Miller.

Thank you for your help.

Laura

From: Al Carpenter
Tue, 2 Jul 2002

Hi Laura!

Nice to hear from you, again! I certainly do remember your name, although I must admit I can't say the same for our limited correspondence those many years ago.

A whole lot has happened to all of us since then - to you, to me, and to our families. I am sorry to hear of the loss of your father - such events can be so devastating - but they are truly an inescapable thread in the fabric of our lives. In the nearly thirty years since I returned home from Vietnam, many such significant and emotional events - some bad, some good - have contributed to who we now are. And so life will continue, until there is no more!

Mine has been largely very good, and I am thankful for that. I hope that yours has been rewarding and happy, too, and that it will continue to be so.

You mentioned your desire to "return" "my" bracelet to me. I am touched by your sentiment, but I will advise you as I have other wearers of my bracelet, from the very first. It is not really "my" bracelet. It has my name on it, but the purpose of it, and of all the P.O.W. bracelets, was to provide a connection, or focus, of purpose and support for the POW's and all of our servicemen and women during those difficult days, months and years of the Vietnam war. It appears, at least in your case, to have served its purpose well.

If you were to return the bracelet to me, it would become one of many, in two shoe boxes I have, each full of bracelets sent to me shortly after I returned home in 1973. I would much prefer that you keep it, as a single, pointed reminder of your involvement in a worthwhile effort when you were very young, and as a direct, unique connection with one American warrior, who sacrificed nearly as much in the service of his country as it is possible to do.

Your support of me and my comrades, and of all that we stood for then, and now be transferred to the new, young American warriors, in places like Afghanistan. They need the moral support of their countrymen now, just as I and my fellow warriors needed it in Vietnam. Be there for them, as you once were for me - and keep that bracelet, so you will never forget me, and the other Americans who help, or have helped, to secure the way of life we all tend to so easily take for granted.

Again, I thank you for your willingness to get involved - and thanks so much, for caring!

Sincerely,

Al

[CDR Allan R. Carpenter, USN (Ret)]
Hanoi, 11/01/66 - 03/04/73

The return to U.S. military control. Parsels, Maj John USA (Ret), saluting.

MADISON, WILLIAM LOUIS
Remains returned 12/13/99

Rank/Branch: E5/U.S. Air Force
Unit: 4th Air Commando Squadron, DaNang Airbase, South Vietnam
Date of Birth: 03 November 1935
Home City of Record: Lexington KY
Date of Loss: 15 May 1966
Country of Loss: Laos
Status (in 1973): Missing In Action
Category: 2
Aircraft/Vehicle/Ground: AC47

From: Macgrory
Date: Tue, 15 Jan 2002 00:19:43 EST

To the family of William L Madison:

I never experienced combat.

However, through my enlistment in the Air Force from 27 June 65 through 4 December 68, my father who was a medic in a field artillery battalion in the South Pacific in World War II, the gentleman (Normandy Invasion) whom my mother married after my father passed way, being a Past Commander of my local American Legion Post, and being a Cincinnati native, I say with love and affection that I was privileged to wear my POW-MIA Bracelet with Sgt. Madison's name inscribed upon it.

We're all older now - we've learned a few things. We now know the price of freedom. Thank you, Bill. Your name will never leave our lips. You are like so many others but yet you are special. We say, "Thank you."

To all Vets.
God Bless you and God Bless America.
Thank you.

DIX, CRAIG MITCHELL
Rank/Branch: E4/U.S. Army
Date of Birth: 05 December 1949 (Trenton MI)
Home City of Record: Livonia MI
Date of Loss: 17 March 1971
Country of Loss: Cambodia
Status (in 1973): Missing In Action
Category: 1
Aircraft/Vehicle/Ground: UH1H

From: Margie Honey
18 Apr 2000

Written For: SSG Craig Mitchell Dix, United States Army

When Freedom Comes

I unwrapped the package when it came in the mail, and found a small bracelet with a man's name and date printed on it. Not a bright shiny bracelet like you might find in a jewelry store or at Macys but a plain silver band, rather dull in color. It was about a quarter inch wide, nothing dainty. A bracelet representing a soldier, Missing in Action since March 17, 1971.

A simple silver band. An embossed name. A date. Will this change anything? I wanted it to make a difference, to send our men home in one piece, and to let freedom be a part of our lives once again.

In 1964 President Johnson got involved in the Vietnam War. He had already sent over 500,000 military troops into the jungles and muddy waters of Vietnam. Our men and women were being taken captive and worse. Rumor had it they were being treated badly, and the American people wanted them to come home. The nation grew restless, and the beginning of the largest anti-war movement in history began.

During that time, someone where I worked had heard there were bracelets being sold for $2.50. I wasn't sure exactly what I was buying, but if it had something positive to do with the war, I was all for it. I couldn't imagine such a small donation doing very much, but it was worth a chance.

My heart stood still as I looked at the bracelet and thought, "Please, let him be alive! And healthy. He has to be healthy - he's a soldier. He'll be in good shape," I reassured myself.

There was an enclosed card, which read in part, "It should be worn with the vow that it will not be removed until the day the Red Cross is allowed into Hanoi and can assure his family of his status and that he receives the humane treatment due all men.

"That sounds good. After all, that is what we wanted, for our soldiers all to return to us unharmed and in good spirits."

I picked up the bracelet and held it tight while I re-read the card. Silently, I made the promise.

Craig Dix. That's his name. It reminds me of someone from the southern states. Maybe South Carolina. Someone who is tall and well built. Not over-built, but a good-sized man. Wavy blonde hair with dark blue eyes, and maybe a medium complexion, one that will tan in the summer months. Or maybe he is a black man. Dark, nappy hair, cropped short, with soft, dark brown eyes that would surely bring a smile to a child's face. A gentle man. One that loved his country. Enough to fight for it.

"March 17, 1971. Missing in action."

No longer could I think of these guys as being gorgeous hunks in their magnificent uniforms-but men. Men who stood for their country and for the safety of the American people. Men we could surely be proud of.

Embracing the curve of the bracelet, I slipped it around my wrist. I rubbed my finger over his name and prayed he would come home. I could feel myself give into the bracelet, as if I knew everything about him, while in reality I knew so little.

"Craig Dix. I like that name!"

Already this had turned out to be more than a bracelet. It had become an article of faith, a matter of principal. At that moment, I succumbed to the idea of having the bracelet and all that it meant. I immortalized the men who fought for our freedom, showing their courage and bravado.

The newspapers and television news reels reported the young people of America were becoming unsettled. They demonstrated against the war, and drugs became the power. These protests brought arrests, which meant little to the disapproving youth, if anything at all. Middle-aged Americans did not understand. The older generation shook their heads in disbelief. The generation gap was in full-swing as the college-age kids pressed on. They burned their draft cards, and finally they burned the flag of the United States!

President Nixon intervened in 1970 and brought some of the men home. We all saw men on stretchers, some in wheel chairs. Others, all broken and bent, walking with the help of crutches. I waited to hear his name on the news, telling me my warrior was safe. I gasped at the reality, but I did not hear his name.

When the survivors did come home from Vietnam, there were no parades. No flagged cars lined up to have our men stand bravely as they had stood in Vietnam. No one threw confetti. No one cheered. There was no one to celebrate the return of the military.

Why? What did it all mean? Could we bring these people back to a normalcy? It seemed as if America would never be the same.

Several years later there was a dedication to the POWs and MIAs. I dreaded the thought that I might see Craig Dix on that program as they listed scores of Army, Navy, Marine, and Air Force personnel, showing roles of names of the dead, bringing them home in flag-draped coffins of red, white and blue. I did not see his flag, nor did I hear his name.

My bracelet saw me through a romance, a baby being born, a marriage, and a family that blossomed. It watched us in celebration as well as in sorrow. It took showers with me, and went through every other phase of my life, faithfully, for over nine years.

I don't remember why I took the bracelet off. But I do remember placing it in my living room. "A place of honor," I recalled, "next to the little house left to me by my Aunt Marge, and some small pictures that are precious to me."

It's been thirty years since I placed my order for the bracelet. Once in a while, I still wear it, but not as often-usually on Memorial Day and the Fourth of July. And sometimes when he's in my thoughts.

Craig Dix. He is a part of me. My personal hero. A man that I will forever honor.

Now they have built the Vietnam Wall, a place in Washington, DC, where thousands of soldiers have been recognized in their own glory and distinction. I long to go there, to see his name enthroned in dedication among the men and women who also lost their lives in this war which made little sense.

When will freedom come? Will I hear something of him?

My questions seemed as simple as the silver band worn around my wrist. Yet, the questions remain - unanswered.

Margie Honey

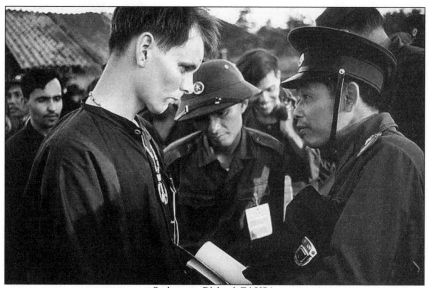

Springman, Richard, E4 USA

HOLLEY, TILDEN STEWART
Rank/Branch: O3/U.S. Air Force
Unit: 389th Tactical Fighter Squadron, Da Nang
Date of Birth: 04 June 1935
Home City of Record: Cameron TX
Date of Loss: 20 January 1968
Country of Loss: North Vietnam
Status (in 1973): Missing in Action
Category: 2
Aircraft/Vehicle/Ground: F4C
Other Personnel in Incident: James A. Ketterer (missing)

From: RICK STUBBLEFIELD
20 Jan 2002

This is my very first e-mail sent to anyone, and I can't think of a better way to start. In my junior year of high school I purchased a POW/MIA bracelet with the name Tilden Holley.

I am forty-five now and was watching a documentary on Vietnam when I thought about my bracelet, which sorry to say I have not worn for years but still have. I went to my computer and did a search on Tildens' name feeling very emotional at the time. When the search results came back, I started crying like a baby because the first name I saw was Holley, Tilden S. To add to the emotion I already had was the fact that he and his backseater, James A. Ketterer were reported MIA on Sunday, 20 Jan., the same day and date I searched his name.

My heart goes out to all families of POW/MIA's who hasn't received any closure after all these years.

Rick Stubblefield

BODDEN, TIMOTHY ROY
Remains Identified 09/08/00

Rank/Branch: E5/U.S. Marine Corps
Unit: HMM 165, Marine Air Group 36
Date of Birth: 06 November 1942
Home City of Record: Downer's Grove IL
Loss Date: 03 June 1967
Country of Loss: Laos
Status (in 1973): Missing In Action
Category: 2
Acft/Vehicle/Ground: CH46A

From: Ray Baker
24 Dec 1999

My name is Ray Baker and I purchased Tim's bracelet in 1971 at NAS Memphis. I have worn it ever since. The "original" has been retired, as I was allergic to it after it wore down to the brass. It broke a couple of times but I had it re-soldered and continued to wear it with a strip of duct tape on the under side to keep it from making a rash on me.

I saw an add in some catalog for POW bracelets about 10 years ago but the company said that it could not honor any requests for a specific name. Price was $19.95. I called them and explained to them that the bracelet that I had was falling apart and that I would gladly pay $50.00 or what ever they needed but I had to have Tim's name. They said they would see what they could do and get back to me. About two weeks later, I got Tim's bracelet in the mail free of charge.

I served in the Marines from 1970 to 1976. Flew Hueys in Nam.

I guess I just wanted to let you know that there is someone in New Mexico that thinks of Tim everyday and prays for your strength.

GOD'S SPEED AND SEMPER FI.

CONDIT, DOUGLAS CRAIG
REMAINS IDENTIFIED 04 JAN 93

Rank/Branch: 02/U.S. Air Force
Date of Birth: 05 February 1942
Home City of Record: Forest Grove OR
Date of Loss: 26 November 1967
Country of Loss: North Vietnam
Status (in 1973): Missing in Action
Category: 2
Aircraft/Vehicle/Ground: F4C
Other Personnel in Incident: Herbert O. Brennan (missing)

BROWN, PAUL GORDON

Rank/Branch: O2/U.S. Marine Corps
Unit: 1 MAW
Date of Birth: 25 August 1943
Home City of Record: Newton MA
Date of Loss: 25 July 1968
Country of Loss: North Vietnam
Status (in 1973): Returnee
Aircraft/Vehicle/Ground: A6A
Other Personnel in Incident: Major Curt Lawson (rescued)

From: Diane Stevens
5 Feb 2002

Captain Douglas Craig Condit was born February 5, 1942 - and today would have been his 60th birthday.

In his memory, I'm leaving this note - still keeping his bracelet that I've had since 1967. He was shot down on my birthday - November 26, 1967.

I also met Paul Brown - a POW - who lives in California. It was in 1986 and what a story he had to tell me as we talked outside the

Snooty Fox Restaurant in El Toro. I'm married to a retired fighter pilot - Marine Corps - who received several citations - one of which was the Distinguished Flying Cross Award.

Today was my first day out of the hospital - in a week, and looking at my notes on the calendar, was this entry "Captain Condit's 60th birthday". So, I figured I had the strength to type up something to remember both Paul Brown and Captain Condit. They endured; suffered - fought bravely, and one lost his life in this effort. If they can do all this, surely I can mark this spot - this day - and ask that you include it in the love-letters you'll receive.

Thank you.

Diane Stevens

Fer, Col. John USAF, (Ret) and Mom

HAWTHORNE, RICHARD WILLIAM

Branch/Rank: O4/U.S.Marine Corps
Unit: VCMJ 1 MAGG 11
Date of Birth: 12 November 1933
Home City of Record: Troy NY
Date of Loss: 12 September 1967
Country of Loss: South Vietnam
Status (in 1973): Presumptive Finding of Death
Category: 4
Aircraft/Vehicle/Ground: RF4B #153104

From: Michele Ward
4 May 2000

For over thirty years I have had a bracelet honoring Major Richard Hawthorne.

From information I have found in his biography, I understand that a PFOD/BNR was issued in 1973. This is six years after the September 12, 1967 date on my bracelet.

This bracelet and this man have been a part of my life for many years. I think of him often and pray for him and his family. I pray for the thousands of young men of my generation who were lost. I pray for those who are still alive out there somewhere. I pray for those who came home un-welcomed and unappreciated. I pray that this nation never again turns its back on the brave and courageous service personnel who protect and defend us when called upon.

I find myself drawn to this site again and again.

And each time I wonder:
did Major Hawthorne have children;
did Major Hawthorne like sports, movies, walking in the rain;
did Major Hawthorne prefer sunsets or sunrises;

did Major Hawthorne enjoy Sunday mornings with the newspaper
and cup of coffee;
did Major Hawthorne glance at the first star each night and make a
wish;
did Major Hawthorne lay on his back in the grass and watch the
clouds;
did Major Hawthorne make angels in the snow;
did he do all those things we take so much for granted every day?
If he did,
I pray he is still doing them somewhere.

To his family:
Always know this - he is loved and remembered by someone who
never knew him but will always be grateful that he lived.

To all the families of those who served:
Always know this - that here is one person who will be eternally
appreciative for the sacrifices that were made and for the gifts that
were given.

With Love and Gratitude,

Michele Ward

Baker, B/Gen David USAF (Ret)

RITTICHIER, JACK C.

Rank/Branch: O3/U.S. Coast Guard
Unit: CG 37 ARRS
Date of Birth: 17 August 1933
Home City of Record: Barberton, OH
Date of Loss: 09 June 1968
Country of Loss: South Vietnam
Status (in 1973): Killed In Action/Body Not Recovered
Category: 3
Aircraft/Vehicle/Ground: HU3E #6714710

From: Janet O'Reilly Herron
7 Jul 2002

Today, July 7, 2002, I placed the bracelet of LT Jack Columbus
Rittichier, MIA, on my wrist. I requested a Coast Guardsman and
was told that LT Jack Rittichier is the only Coast Guardsman who
has not come home.

I have been able to find some information about the circumstances
which led to LT Rittichier's never coming home and his heroic
efforts to save his fellow troops. I am grateful that I am able to
know something about the brave man whose name I now wear".

I am ashamed that our government has forgotten LT Rittichier. I
pray that LT Rittichier's family will find my note - I want them to
know I share their hopes, sorrow, and love, for LT Rittichier. I will
hold them in prayer always.

God bless all of you. Any veteran that may read this, I want to
thank you for your service in keeping my family and I free and
safe.

Welcome Home.

Janet

GOURLEY, LAURENT LEE

Rank/Branch: O3/U.S. Air Force
Unit: 416th Tactical Fighter Squadron, Tuy Hoa Airbase, SVN
Date of Birth: 05 September 1944
Home City of Record: Villisco IA
Date of Loss: 09 August 1969
Country of Loss: Laos
Status (in 1973): Missing In Action
Category: 4
Acft/Vehicle/Ground: F100F

From: Mary Adolph
21 Sep 1998

To the family of Capt. Gourley

I sent for a POW bracelet back in 1971. I was 20 years old and working midnights as a nurses aid at a local hospital. I was sleeping when the mail came and my roommate threw the package on my bed and said your bracelet finally came. Half asleep I looked at the name on the bracelet and went back to sleep. When I woke up I thought I had dreamt about the bracelet until I saw the package at the foot of my bed. It still amazes me that I received Lee's bracelet because my mother's maiden name was Gourley. It was even more special to me because I thought maybe we were related. I wore it for years and only took it off only when I had to during Nurses training. I have always wondered what happening to my POW. Anytime there was anything printed about Men returned home or any information about them I would look for his name. I never wanted it to be on the remains or confirmed dead list. Yesterday I read in our local news paper about this web site and decided to see what I could find. It saddened me to see that we still don't know. My children are both in High School and are taking a new course offered this year called "The Vietnam Era" so they have been asking me lots of questions and I was asked to wear my bracelet to show their class. Talking to them about that war is still painful and it's so hard to make them understand how it affected all of us. I really hope that you know that he is not forgotten. Thank you.

Mary Adolph

CUNNINGHAM, KENNETH LEROY

Rank/Branch: E2/U.S. Army
Unit: 225th Aviation Company, 223rd Aviation Battalion, 17th
Aviation Group, 1st Aviation Brigade
Date of Birth: 21 January 1948 (Olney IL)
Home City of Record: Ellery IL
Date of Loss: 03 October 1969
Country of Loss: South Vietnam
Status (in 1973): Missing In Action
Category: 4
Acft/Vehicle/Ground: OV1C
Other Personnel In Incident: Paul L. Graffe (missing)

From: Donna Arfmann
12 Feb 2002

In 1971 I was a 14 year old girl that was deeply affected by the issue of missing American soldiers in Vietnam, Laos and Cambodia. I bought a POW bracelet and wore it every day for years. My wrist sometimes turned a greenish color but it didn't matter. I was certain that some day I would be able to give that bracelet to the man its name bore. When the POWs returned home I feverishly checked the lists in the newspapers and was saddened to not find his name listed. I still held out hope that some day he would return and I would be able to give him that worn bracelet and say "Welcome Home." From time to time I see an article in the paper or hear a newscast about a returning POW or the repatriated remains and check to see if it's him. Although I no longer wear the bracelet daily I'll never forget the name of the young man engraved on it.

Today I was watching a local news show and there was a segment on POWs. To my dismay I found that there is still no definitive information on "my" POW.

I'm now 44 years old and the mother of an 18 year-old son who has enlisted in the Air Force and will be leaving home soon after high school graduation in June. My thoughts went to the mother of "my" POW who has been waiting since 1969 for word on her son's status. My thoughts and prayers are with her and all members of his family. He may have been married and had children.....I don't know. I hope he lived alot in the 21 years before his aircraft crashed in Southeast Vietnam.

"My" POW is Kenneth Cunningham, lost 10/3/69 in S. Vietnam. I still have his bracelet and will continue to treasure it until there's an answer to his whereabouts. I'll do whatever I can to ease their grief and help celebrate his life.

My thoughts and prayers are with the Cunningham family and all families of the still unaccounted for POWs and MIAs.

Donna Arfmann

Returnees Unknown

TOOMEY, SAMUEL KAMU III
Remains Returned - ID Announced 08 February 1990

Rank/Branch: O4/U.S. Army
Unit: Armor, Special Operations Group, Headquarters, MACV-
SOG, (some accounts list Toomey as "Special Missions Officer")
Date of Birth: 30 December 1935 (Honolulu HI)
Home City of Record: Independence MO
Date of Loss: 30 November 1968
Country of Loss: Laos
Status (in 1973): Missing In Action
Category: 4

From: T. R. Isaacs, Jr.
13 Jul 1999

To the family of Samuel K. Toomey:

I knew Sam... I remember him as being tall, broad shoulder, olive
skinned. I remember arm wrestling with him in the "O Club" at CCN,
with Col Warren and another Major that was the S-3 (Operations
officer) Sam was the Ass't S-3. He was a super fine officer, and a good
man.

The mission Sam went on was a prisoner snatch and Italian Green
mission... where we planted booby-trapped weapons and ammunition for
the enemy.

I had thirty days to go in country and should have been on that mission
instead of Sam. I was picked but because I only had thirty days left, Sam
requested to go in my place. He had not been on a mission before.

I owe my life to Samuel K. Toomey. I will always love him and keep
him in my prayers. Whenever I go to D.C., I make sure I stop by the
Wall to say hello, and talk to him. Samuel K. Toomey will never be
forgotten.

T. R. Isaacs, Jr.

SHIVELY, JAMES RICHARD
Rank/Branch: O2/U.S. Air Force
Home City of Record: Spokane WA
Date of Loss: 05-May-67
Country of Loss: North Vietnam
Status (in 1973): Returnee
Aircraft/Vehicle/Ground: F105D

From: Jane Welsh
2 May 2002

On May 5
Sad day then
Glad day now
Thank you for your bravery
You are not forgotten
Your name is worn with honor
Fondly.
jane welsh

Cronin, Capt. Michael J. USNR (Ret)

RAUSCH, ROBERT ERNEST

Rank/Branch: O3/U.S. Air Force
Unit: 12th Tactical Reconnaissance Squadron
Date of Birth: 22 May 1938
Home City of Record: Hicksville NY
Date of Loss: 16 April 1970
Country of Loss: Laos
Status (in 1973): Missing in Action
Category: 4
Acft/Vehicle/Ground: RF4C
Other Personnel in Incident: Richard L. Ayers (missing)

From: Gisin, Marilynne
26 Apr 2002

Hello....

I just discovered this site today and am overcome by emotion.

In 1971, as a girl in my 20's in Washington, DC, I became the proud but sad owner of a POW bracelet with (at that time) Capt. Robert E. Rausch's name and hometown. I was a White House staffer at the time in the Nixon Administration and remembered one day being called in by a Director who asked that I remove this bracelet for it was a "liberal" act against the Administration. I responded that the Vice President had just planted a tree on behalf of the POWs and MIAs and I saw no difference between my action and his. I continued to wear the bracelet for seven years through labor, birth and delivery of my daughter and, in general, my life.

I looked down one day in the late '70's and discovered it had broken apart and was gone. I was bereft. I didn't want to choose another soldier -- Capt. Rausch was my soldier. So I've kept him in my prayers for these many years and there's hardly a day that goes by I don't think of him and his bravery on behalf of his country.

As I said, I discovered this site and was able to obtain information on his biography and details of his capture. For this, I'm very grateful. This afternoon I ordered another bracelet (stainless steel) with the Major's name inscribed. It will serve as a constant reminder that in this new century we're only here because of Robert Rausch and the others like him who went into service on behalf of their country and are still, quite possibly, out there.

Sincerely,

Marilynne

Families, friends and news crews greeted each group of returnees

WARNER, JAMES HOWIE
Rank/Branch: O2/U.S. Marine Corps, EWO
Unit: VMFA 323
Date of Birth: 26 February 1941
Home City of Record: Ypisalanti MI
Date of Loss: 13 October 67
Country of Loss: North Vietnam
Status (in 1973): Returnee
Aircraft/Vehicle/Ground: F4B, tail #150477

From: David Cannon
7 May 2000

I wish to say thank you to the greatest heroes of my youth. My grandmother on my mother's side had 7 brothers, a son and a son-in-law who all served in WW2. My own father is a Korean War Vet (U.S. Navy) and I myself served in the Navy 1978-1984. I feel very fortunate that all of those in my family who served in WW2, Korea, and Viet Nam, as well as the more recent Gulf War, were able to return home to their family.

Many families were less fortunate and my heart goes out to them. As a young boy growing up in the late 60's and early 70's I watched with great interest the events and exploits of our men in Vietnam. Like many I was troubled by the lack of welcome they saw if and when they returned. That to me is the greater tragedy of Vietnam. It was the courage and determination of returning Vets who came home and made a success of themselves that inspired me in part to join the Navy when I turned 18. U believe that much of what is great about America in the past 100 years was built by the men who fought in all of its wars. It is a monument to those who came home to us, and to those who still remain unreturned.

I collect militaria as a way to preserve, protect, and maintain a connection to this under-recognized part of American History. It was part of the research I conduct on each and every artifact which brought me to this site. Much thanks to the people who created, and continue to maintain this site, and greater thanks to the Vets and their families to whom no high enough honor can ever repay the cost they willingly paid for freedom.

The great American whom I was researching was Marine Capt. James Howie Warner 10-13-67. He was one of the very fortunate, a POW returnee. It was the recent purchase of his POW/MIA bracelet which sparked my interest. I had reason to believe that it was an original due to a reasonable amount of wear on it's inner surface. Now I am sure of it. His bio from this site, along with this bracelet will serve to me as a reminder of the many who did not come home to us. I wish I could know more about the person who wore this bracelet so faithfully, and of the man whose return it symbolizes.

I salute you, Capt. Warner.

David

Seek, Col. Brian USAF (Ret)

LUNA, JOSE DAVID
Rank/Branch: O3/U.S. Air Force
Home City of Record: Orange CA
Date of Loss: 10 March 1967
Country of Loss: North Vietnam
Status (in 1973): Returnee
Aircraft/Vehicle/Ground: F105F #8335
Other Personnel in Incident: David Everson, returnee

From: Mark Smith
06 Jun 2000

Dear Colonel Luna:

My name is Mark Smith. That probably doesn't sound familiar to you but I'm sure you'll remember me. I was 12 years old in 1973. I had worn your POW bracelet for several years. My father was a Chief Master Sergeant in the Air Force stationed at Travis AFB.

I got out of school one day because my mother found out you were coming back from Vietnam on the flight that day. We went to Travis to meet the plane. I tried talking to several security police officers about letting me give the bracelet to you. They all said I wouldn't be able to get near you or the plane. My mom and her friend put me up to just running out to the plane and giving it to you when you got off the plane. My dad was there at the time and he didn't know anything about it. He wasn't too happy with my mom for encouraging me to do that.

Anyway, when I heard your name called I ran out there and gave you the bracelet. I was too nervous to remember what you said but I think you shook my hand and said thank you.

You and I made the front page of the local papers the next day and got a mention on the local news and I think even the national news. Anyway, I was twelve years old then. I'm 38 now. I joined the Air Force Reserve when I was 18 and became a Loadmaster on the C-141. That was almost 20 years ago. In about 1982 or so I flew a leg of a mission from Hawaii back to Travis carrying the remains of six MIA's that were being returned from Vietnam. I don't know if you recall that particular mission or not but our plane was on the cover of Time magazine that week sitting on the tarmac at Travis in about the same location your plane had arrived. I'm not visible in the picture but I was on the loading ramp of the plane as the coffins were being carried off the plane.

I became a police officer while I was in the Air Force reserve and have been doing that for almost 17 years now. I was a police officer in Fairfield which is the city that Travis AFB is located. I got shot in the stomach in 1989 by a drug dealer and nearly died. I ended up retiring from the City force and now I work as a Detective for the Stanislaus County District Attorney, which is in Modesto California.

I thought you just may want to know whatever happened to that little kid that was one of the first things you saw as you arrived back at the mainland after your ordeal in Vietnam. I'm glad you made it home safe and according to the web page you retired as a Lt. Col so I'm guessing you stayed in the Air Force for a while longer after you got back. Hope things are going well for you.

Sincerely,
Mark Smith

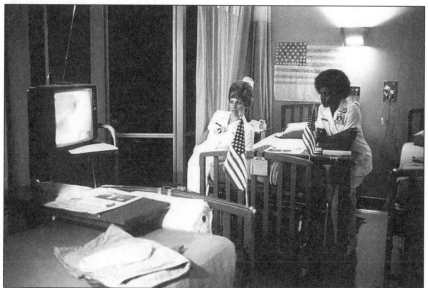
Hospital staff awaits the arrival of the returnees

CROSBY, HERBERT CHARLES
Rank/Branch: O3/U.S. Army
Unit: 71st Aviation Company, 14th Aviation Battalion, 16th
Aviation Group, 23rd Infantry Division (Americal), Chu Lai
Date of Birth: 30 May 1947 (Ft. Wayne IN)
Home City of Record: South Georgia
Date of Loss: 10 January 1970
Country of Loss: South Vietnam
Status (in 1973): Missing In Action
Category: 4
Acft/Vehicle/Ground: UH1C, "Firebirds"

From: Theresa S. Saunders
26 Dec 1999

My first consciousness of the injustice of the Vietnam war
occurred in my freshman year of high school, (1972-73) when a
friend began volunteering to distribute POW bracelets and collect
donations. I received Capt. Crosby's (if my memory serves, for
the donation of one dollar) and soon after began distributing them
myself. I wore it throughout most of high school removing it, I
believe when the war was over. I wish I had been more true to my
pledge of wearing it until the fate of Capt. Crosby was known.
However, it has never been far from my notice, kept in a jewelry
box where I often removed it and thought of him and his family.

I have discovered from this web site that he is still listed as missing
in action. I have a son who is only a couple of years younger than
Capt. Crosby when he was lost. I cannot imagine the pain of going
all these years without the knowledge of what had really happened
to my child.

The bracelet is out of the box now and back on my arm.

Sincerely,

T. Sharon Saunders

TOLBERT, CLARENCE ORFIELD
Remains Returned November 3, 1988

Rank/Branch: O6/U.S. Navy
Unit: Attack Squadron 56, USS Midway (CVA-41)
Date of Birth: 04 June 1939
Home City of Record: Tishomingo OK
Date of Loss: 06 November 1972
Country of Loss: North Vietnam
Status (in 1973): Missing In Action
Category: 2
Aircraft/Vehicle/Ground: A7B

From: Beth Branch
11 May 1999

I knew him as a young midshipman at Annapolis. He was my first love. All he wanted to do was fly. I will never forget him.

Webber

Harris, Col. Carlisle "Smitty" USAF (Ret)

KEAVENEY, THOMAS ROBERT

MILITARY SERVICE	ARMY
COUNTRY OF CASUALTY	SOUTH VIETNAM
TYPE OF CASUALTY	HOSTILE KILLED
RANK	PFC
PAY GRADE	E3
CASUALTY DATE	01/18/67
HOME OF RECORD	NEW YORK, NEW YORK
DATE OF BIRTH	04/22/45
CAUSE	EXPLOSIVE DEVICE
AIR / NO AIR	GROUND CASUALTY

From: Leriche Yvan
15 May 2002

To all of you, Vietnam's Veterans - In your memory.

Today, at the age of 40, I have often read about the 39-45 war. With time, I discovered another war, the Vietnam War and since then, I just cannot break away from it!!! But what I discovered the most is, a lost, American youth, destroyed and so profoundly touched by the events. And over the years, I realized the extend of this disaster, leaving behind some indelible scars... they are painful, fragile and touchy.

Although I collect all kinds of documentaries on the Vietnam War, there are two of them that I keep preciously and carefully because I need them. They, in fact, allow me to share with you some emotion... Your emotion. These documents are: "Platoon Anderson" and "Dear America". I watch them as often as I can and some names, like Padilla the ranchero, Kevin Macauley and the very young Keaveney of New York, are carved in my mind. But of course, there is also William Reed Stock. His mother wrote a letter that moved me tremendously. Nevertheless, I do not and will never forget the others, the heroes without any names.

With Internet, I was able to find many veterans. Unfortunately, since I am a French speaking man, and do not master the English language very well, I have some difficulties to understand what I am discovering and most of all what I want to express. But I know that whatever I understand touches me deeply. For this reason, I promised myself to take some intensive English courses. These lessons will also be an asset for me when, one day, in a very near future, I will finally go to this Big Black Wall, where 50,000 names are engraved. There, I will quietly meditate.

I would certainly love to offer a flower for the memories of Padilla, John Wilson, William Reed Stock, without forgetting Sharon Ann Lane... this beautiful young nurse.

I am also planning on visiting the Brooklyn's Cemetery in order to put a bouquet of flowers on Keaveney's grave...this young boy whose face I was able to discover through the documents I have seen and read... Somehow, I miss him so much! It is about all for now. In front of all of you, Veterans, I bow with the utmost respect.

And I would like you to know that I will always have some thoughts and feelings for you. God bless you. Peace.

Yvan Leriche

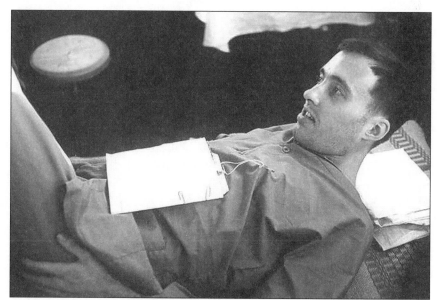

Baker, B/Gen David USAF (Ret)

BAILEY, JAMES WILLIAM
Rank/Branch: O2/U.S. Navy
Unit: Fighter Squadron 143, USS Constellation
Date of Birth: 19 January 1943
Home City of Record: Kosciusko MS
Date of Loss: 28 June 1967
Country of Loss: North Vietnam
Status (in 1973): Released POW
Aircraft/Vehicle/Ground: F4B
Missions: 183
Other Personnel in Incident: William P. Lawrence (released POW)

From: Valerie Daugherty
15 Jun 2000

To: Lt. James W. Bailey, USN, (Hometown, Kosciusko, Mississippi)

So many years have gone by now, but you are still in my mind and in my heart. For years I have carried a feeling of regret for not seeking you out as I should have. You see, I came so very close to actually meeting you--you were so close but Secret Service agents prevented me from being able to personally hand you the P.O.W. bracelet that I had worn for almost three years without ever taking it off. I remember so clearly that day in Meridian, Mississippi as President and Mrs. Nixon came to N.A.S. Meridian to dedicate the new Stennis Training Center. I arrived several hours early in order to get a seat as close as possible to the stage. Upon your arrival, I pushed my way through the crowd and as a Secret Service agent told me to move back, I took off my bracelet and asked him to give it to you. I can still see you smiling and waving as I blew you a kiss. You had become a very big part of my life as I prayed fervently to God every day for your safe return and I still thank Him for answering my prayers. I'd like you to also know that I did have the distinct pleasure of actually meeting your mother as she was driven to N.A.S. Memphis to meet you upon your return home. My husband and I had stopped for gas in Vaiden, Mississippi as we traveled home to Memphis and I noticed a gray

Navy sedan at the station with an elderly lady in the backseat. I told my husband that I felt that it was your mother, so I went to the car and introduced myself to her.   So you see, I came very close to almost meeting you.

Lt. Bailey, for years now I have wanted to just thank you for the sacrifice you made during your imprisonment for the precious gift of freedom that we as Americans have enjoyed and that have been extended to my children and now my two grandchildren. You are indeed a hero and truly the "wind beneath our wings".

Very sincerely,

Valerie Daugherty

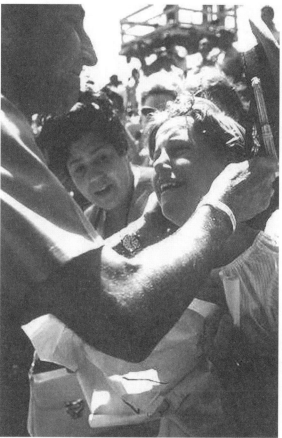

Mullens, Capt. Richard "Moon" USN (Ret) and his bracelet wearer,
Debra Davis Howard, at Clark Air Force Base.

WILLIAMS, HOWARD KEITH
REMAINS IDENTIFIED 26 FEB 92

Rank/Branch: O3/U.S. Air Force
Date of Birth: 25 October 1936
Home City of Record: Stubenville OH
Date of Loss: 18 March 1968
Country of Loss: North Vietnam
Status (in 1973): Missing in Action
Category: 2
Aircraft/Vehicle/Ground: F100F

From: Patsy Smith
30 Sep 1998

To the family of Major Howard Keith Williams....

Please know I have faithfully kept Maj. Howard's bracelet all these years. Many days passed between 3-18-68 to 012/96.... all, I know, in heartache. Our first-born son was born 7-22-68 and his father left for Viet Nam 5 weeks later. He did return and we are here 30 years later. The irony of this to me is our connection with your family with the bracelets and the dates for April 3, 1996, our first-born son's beautiful wife and 48 day old daughter were killed by a drunk driver. 1968 and 1996 years of joy and heartache. Thank heaven for the joys which sustain us.

I have Maj. William's bracelet but I know it is yours. It is rubbed down because with almost every prayer I said for him and his family I was holding the bracelet or it was on my wrist. It is on my wrist as I write this to you now. I am thankful I found this site which is in a link from a drunk driving victim's site...yet again another painful connection.

I know he is at peace as are our Laurie and Mary Witten. God's peace and love to you.

Patsy Fisher Smith

BOGGS, PASCHAL GLENN

Rank/Branch: O3/U.S. Marine Corps
Unit: VMA 533 MAG 12
Date of Birth: 07 March 1936
Home City of Record: EAST POINT GA
Date of Loss: 27 August 1967
Country of Loss: North Vietnam Over Water
Status (in 1973): Presumptive Finding of Death
Category: 5
Aircraft/Vehicle/Ground: A6A
Other Personnel in Incident: Vladimir Bacik, missing

From: Laura Garcia
28 May 2002

Memorial Day 2002 has just ended - a more reflective, introspective Memorial Day in the aftermath of Sept. 11th. I planted three trees this morning in memory of the victims/heroes at each site - Pennsylvania, New York City, and Washington D.C. My thoughts then turned to the bracelet I wear each Memorial Day, 4th of July & Veteran's Day which bears the name of another hero - Maj. Paschal G. Boggs. I had found out his hometown years ago at the Vietnam Memorial, but knew little else about him. Thank you for enabling me to add more pieces to the vague picture.

I received my bracelet in the early 1970's while I was in high school. It was a common unifying bond for the polarized society of the time. I wore it constantly through high school and then on the three holidays, but it was never forgotten.

I thought my bracelet was gone forever eight years ago when my home burned to the ground. In the ashes of one room, I came across the charred remains of the box it resided in - one of the very few possessions that survived. Inside, the bracelet was encrusted black and unrecognizable, but I took it to be cleaned anyway. It came back clean and bright as if it had to remain a memorial to a remarkable man. Thank you,

Laura Garcia

LOHEED, HUBERT BRADFORD
Remains Identified August 23, 1994

Rank/Branch: O5/U.S. Navy
Unit: Commanding Officer, Attack Squadron 146, USS Ranger (CVA 61)
Date of Birth: 15 October 1924 (Brockton MA)
Home City of Record: Middleboro MA
Date of Loss: 01 February 1966
Country of Loss: North Vietnam/Over Water
Status (in 1973): Missing In Action
Category: 3
Aircraft/Vehicle/Ground: A4C

From: Carol Mack
1 Jun 2002

I wore a bracelet for many years with the name of Hubert B. Bradford, who was listed as MIA. I had even received a hand-written letter from a family member, although I no longer remember who.

Unfortunately, I was forced to remove the bracelet when I had my third operation in 1976. I was promised they would put it back on in the recovery room, but, somehow, it was lost. By that time, I no longer knew how to get a replacement, and went on with my life, but I never forgot about him!

For a few years I did receive a sort of newspaper which updated the issues for the POWS/MIAS and their families. It also contained an updated list in each issue of those who had been accounted for. I always searched for Hubert B. Bradford's name, but never found it.

I can no longer remember the branch of service he was in, but I do remember that the letter I had received when I first got the bracelet said that he had been shot down, I think it might have been fairly early in the war.

I seem to remember that he had quite a few years in the service, and he was definitely married and had a few children, but I no longer remember how many.

I know for sure that Hubert B. Bradford is the correct name, as I have NEVER forgotten it!! I have checked your index, but his name is not on it, and I was hoping that you could give me some updated information about him.

I would assume by now that he has been declared Killed In Action, but I would just really like to know as it was an important part of my life - wearing his bracelet. I even had the special little sticker on it that designated him as MIA.

When my friend first got me my bracelet, I was so proud to wear it, and we used to try to get other classmates to wear the bracelets - we were only in 9th grade at the time, and were the first in our graduating class of 1976 to wear them.

I was so jealous of her when her "guy" was only listed as POW, and mine was listed as MIA, because I just knew that meant that mine was NOT coming home. I know what that meant for me - a stranger just wearing his name on a bracelet, I cannot conceive of what that horror was to his family and has been all of these years!

Still, I would really like to know whatever became of his case. I would appreciate any help you could give me!

3 Jun 2002

I would like to thank you for getting back in touch with me so quickly!

I do not remember the name Loheed, but it would only seem logical that it be the correct name when I did have the rest of it correctly. Besides, I doubt there were many other "Hubert Bradfords" who went to Viet Nam, although the numbers who did go and those who did not return is staggering!

How in the world did you ever figure it out? I was really too young at the time to understand all of the political garbage that was attached to the war, but my family has always been a military family. I, myself, had always planned for a career in the Navy, but because of my health issues, no branch of the service would accept me.

I currently have a son in the Navy, and my daughter, only 16, is in the JR. Navy ROTC in her high school. I am proud of both of my children, and we are all very proud to be Americans, and to stand behind our country in peace time, and war time.

I was glad to see the country rally behind our men and women during the Gulf War, and once again after 9/11.

It is also comforting to me as the parent of a sailor, that there will never again be an unknown soldier since they maintain a DNA file on all of our enlisted heroes - and that's what they all are. Most people don't realize the sacrifice they and all of their families make to serve our country. But, again, as the parent of a sailor, I know that every one of them considers it an honor to serve their country.

Thank you for your time, and for your quick response!
Sincerely,

Carol Mack

Adkins, Maj. Clodean USA (Ret) deceased (CIV)

HANLEY, TERRENCE HIGGINS
Rank/Branch: O2/U.S. Navy
Unit: Heavy Photographic Squadron 61, USS Oriskany (CVA-34)
Date of Birth: 16 March 1942
City of Record: Gardiner ME
Date of Loss: 01 January 1968
Country of Loss: North Vietnam/Over Water
Status (in 1973): Missing In Action
Category: 5
Acft/Vehicle/Ground: RA3B

From: John Pusieski
12 Jun 2002

To the family of Lt Terrence H Hanley,

I just wanted you to know that Terrence has been my constant companion for the past 30 years. He has been with me through thick and thin. He has traveled with me to Europe, Mexico, and Canada. He has cruised the waters of the south seas, and visited the northernmost point of Alaska. He has strolled the sunny beaches of Hawaii, and wept with me at the wall. Together, we have honored the memory of Naval heroes of the past from the decks of the "Mighty Mo" and the Arizona memorial. We have strolled the battlefields of the civil war, and the parade grounds of the Naval Academy. We paused to remember in Arlington, and were honored to actually sail aboard "Old Ironsides" in Boston Harbor. Together, we have traveled this country from coast to coast, boarder to boarder. We have served many volunteer organizations, and filled leadership positions most of our time together. We have been married twice, and have 3 wonderful kids. The bracelet that I wear is now very hard to read, but it has never left my wrist. Terrence is remembered and honored every day of my life. He is so much more than a bracelet to me, he is my friend and comrade. I mourn with you his loss, yet celebrate him with life. I am one of the lucky ones that God so far has granted 53 years. It has been an honor to share the last 30 with your Son, Husband & Father. I assure you his memory, and that of all who gave so much will live on in me for whatever is left of my life. God bless you, and grant you peace.

John

LIGON, VERN P. Jr.   Deceased
Rank/Branch: O5/U.S. Air Force
Date of Birth: 04 July 1921
Home City of Record: Frankfort KY
Date of Loss: 19 Nov 1967
Country of Loss: North Vietnam
Status (in 1973): Returnee
Aircraft/Vehicle/Ground: RF4C
> Shot down in WWII in a P 47 on his 26th Mission, 22 April 1944 Held until April 1945 in Germany. Escaped once, recaptured.

ANSHUS, RICHARD C.
Rank/Branch: O2/U.S. Army
Unit: HHC2/1 196th INF BDE
Date of Birth: 29 November 1947
Home City of Record: Minneapolis MN
Date of Loss: 08 March 1971
Country of Loss: South Vietnam/North Vietnam
Status (in 1973): Returnee
Aircraft/Vehicle/Ground: H6A

WILLIAMS, JAMES WESLEY
Rank/Branch: O3/U.S. Air Force
Unit: 432nd Reconnaissance Wing at Udorn AFB
Date of Birth: 31 August 1944 Memphis TN
Home City of Record: Memphis TN
Date of Loss: 20 May 1972
Country of Loss: North Vietnam
Status (in 1973): Returnee
Aircraft/Vehicle/Ground: F4D
Missions: 228

HATCHER, DAVID BURNETT
Branch/Rank: O3/U.S. Air Force
Unit: 333 TFS
Home City of Record: MT. Airy NC
Date of Loss: 30-May-66
Country of Loss: North Vietnam
Status (in 1973): Returnee
Aircraft/Vehicle/Ground: F105
Missions: 87

From, Karene Butler
April 19, 2002

My name is Karene Owens Butler. I am 40 years old next week and 29 years ago at the age of 11 I had the honor of being at Clark AFB in the Philippines when the POW's returned from Vietnam.

In searching names of POWs on your site, I am sad to find that one of the POWs whose bracelet my mother wore and whom she did meet that day, Vernon Ligon is now deceased. My thoughts and heartfelt sorrow go out to his family.

I am also looking to hopefully make contact with 3 other returnees. The first is Retired LtCol Richard C. Anshus. I have a picture of him and myself taken 29 years ago on the flight line at Clark AFB the day he stepped off that plane a free man once again.

I am also looking for Retired LtCol. James W. Williams who I understand resides in Georgia. I also have a picture of my youngest brother who at that time wore his bracelet and was 4 years old. The picture is of my little brother (James William Owens) kissing him right on the lips when he departed from that plane. It was a very heartwarming day not only for me but all who were there to greet the returnees.

Last but certainly not least, Retired LtCol. David Burnett Hatcher. I believe that LtCol. Hatcher was not only a returning POW after 7 years of captivity but a friend of my fathers as well. I have a picture of him, his wife and his 2 daughters that I understand was sent to my parents upon his return to Mt. Airy, NC.

Any help that you or anyone who may read this can give me would be greatly appreciated.

Thank you,

Karene Butler

QUINN, MICHAEL EDWARD
Rank/Branch: O3/U.S. Navy
Unit: Attack Squadron 196, USS Ranger (CVA 61)
Date of Birth: 21 August 1933
Home City of Record: Madelia MN
Date of Loss: 22 November 1969
Country of Loss: Laos
Status (in 1973): Missing In Action
Category: 4
Acft/Vehicle/Ground: A6A

HALL, HARLEY HUBERT
REMAINS RETURNED 06/95 (I.D. disputed)

Rank/Branch: O5/U.S. Navy, pilot
Unit: Fighter Squadron 143, USS Enterprise (CV-65)
Date of Birth: 23 December 1937 (Broken Bow NE)
Home City of Record: Vancouver WA
Date of Loss: 27 January 1973
Country of Loss: South Vietnam
Status (in 1973): Prisoner of War
Category: 1
Acft/Vehicle/Ground: F4J

From: William Horning
26 Jun 2000

TO THE FAMILIES OF MICHAEL QUINN AND HARLEY HALL

Having been born in 1969, I'm the son of a Vietnam vet. My dad never talked much about his tour, still doesn't. I spent much of my formative years pouring over his cruise book from USS Enterprise. Being generally nuts about flying anyway, Naval Aviation became almost an obsession. Bad eyesight, combined with a decided unwillingness to exercise caused any future there to evaporate. I always read a lot about it though, and since Viet Nam was recent enough for me to have vague memories I focused fairly heavily there.

When I was in High School the National League of Families had a table set up in a local mall. I was drawn to them, and decided to purchase a bracelet. I picked Michael E. Quinn. A-6's were a favorite, & it had to be an aviator.

I wore that red aluminum bracelet for 6 years, with the last few being encased in plastic hospital bracelets. The acid in my sweat from southern Arizona summers had dissolved the bracelet, creating sharp points on the ends that had a tendency to draw blood. When I moved to Maryland in 1990, one of my first priorities was going to the Wall. I wasn't sure what to do about my bracelet as it was fast becoming a health hazard! When I got to the Wall and did my rubbing, something clicked and I decided it would be appropriate for me to leave it there. I didn't know what else to do, and I decided that it would be more honorable to leave it there, rather than have it collecting dust in a box somewhere. Before leaving it though, I went to one of the booths nearby and purchased my second bracelet, Harley Hall. Again, a Navy pilot and even from the Big E. I got stainless this time, hoping to avert the same fate as my first. I have never forgotten Michael Quinn, and he will always be a part of me.

A year or two later, my parents were entertaining friends. They wanted to tour the Smithsonian. Mike is a vet, and I knew of the exhibit of artifacts left at the Wall. That was high on our list. While walking through the exhibit, I saw the bracelet display. I started to look through it, saying 'no, never happen.' As I looked, my eyes drifted downward to a Plexiglas stand......with a rubbing that had a bracelet stuck through it. I can't begin to describe the feelings running through me as it dawned that, yes, that was my old bracelet. I still get chills some 6 or 7 years later.

My second bracelet will also be my last. I will never take it off, and at my death it will be returned to the Wall along with part of my ashes, to represent those of us who were lucky enough to know our dads and have enough love to bear someone else's burden.

William Horning

SKINNER, OWEN GEORGE
Rank/Branch: O4/U.S. Air Force
Unit: 23rd Tactical Air Support Squadron, Nakhon Phanom
Airport, Thailand
Date of Birth: 18 November 1933
Home City of Record: Lima OH
Date of Loss: 12 December 1970
Country of Loss: Laos
Status (in 1973): Missing In Action
Category: 2
Acft/Vehicle/Ground: O2A
Other Personnel In Incident: Thomas A. Duckett (missing)

From: Barbara Layne
11 Oct 1998

To the family of Owen Skinner,

In 1971 I was a 19 year old student at the University of Washington, and sent in my $5.00 for a MIA/POW bracelet. I received a stainless steel band with the name of Owen Skinner 12-12-70. I was concerned for his family--did he have a wife? children? and was saddened to note that he was lost just before Christmas.

I wore the band for many years, until it broke. (I have a terribly thin wrist, which required a lot of bending in order to stay on.) Since then, the bracelet has followed me to various cities throughout the U.S. and now, in Montreal Quebec, where the two pieces reside on my bookshelf.

Although I had stopped wearing the bracelet long ago, I continued to wonder about, and hope for the best for Owen Skinner. Last year, I found the web pages which list the status of MIA/POWs and was sorry to learn that Owen Skinner has not been found.

Now, when I consider the worn areas on the bracelet, I remember how young and naive I was in the early 70's....I had several young friends who went to fight, and we were fortunate that they all returned physically unharmed. (Although no one returned unchanged). For me, the significance of the bracelet has increased in time. It reminds me that not everyone made it back, and that each POW/MIA has a name, has a family who loves and misses them. I now check Owen's status report regularly....still concerned, still wondering, still harboring a bit of hope. It is always an emotional experience for me.

I would like to think there is some consolation for you to know that someone else--albeit a stranger--also cares. I send you warmest wishes.

Barbara Layne

Flynn, LtGen. John Peter USAF (Ret), deceased

EGAN, JAMES THOMAS JR.

Rank/Branch: O2/U.S. Marine Corps
Unit: H/3/12
Date of Birth: 31 May 1943
Home City of Record: Mountainside NJ
Date of Loss: 21 January 1966
Country of Loss: South Vietnam
Status (in 1973): Missing In Action
Category: 2
Acft/Vehicle/Ground: Ground

*From: **Suzy Turner***
11 Jul 2000

To the Family of James T. Egan:

I've had Capt. Egan's bracelet for close to 20 years (I now know he was promoted to Major). Until last week, I knew only that he was MIA 1/21/66. I stumbled onto the Moving Memorial Wall in Myrtle Beach, SC, on July 4th. That one "stumble" began an intense search on my part for information on James T. Egan -- and made July 4th, 2000 my most memorable Independence Day of my 41 years.

While at the Moving Wall, I discovered that Maj. Egan is a Marine, so is my Father. My Father was in Vietnam in 1966 and again in 1970. I had quit wearing Maj. Egan's bracelet about 1977 when I no longer heard anything about the POW/MIAs of the Vietnam war and did not know how to contact any organization to stay in touch. But I NEVER forgot Maj. Egan and have continued to pray for him and his family for many, many years.

I called my Father last week, July 4th, and told him what I discovered about my MIA (I still consider Maj. Egan "my" MIA) -- and discovered they strong possibility that Maj. Egan's division was the division performing patrol for the base at which my Father was stationed in Vietnam in 1966. The possibility that Maj. Egan became MIA while protecting my Father struck me hard and cold and I cried.

I will continue to search for information, and hopefully a picture, of Maj. James Egan. I will continue to pray for him and his family. And I will always regard him as my hero and as possibly my Father's guardian angel in Vietnam.

To Maj. Egan's family, I am so sorry for the events of that night and wish I could change them. I would enjoy communicating with you but hold your privacy in the greatest of respect. If we should somehow reach each other, I will be grateful, if not, know that Maj. Egan is more than a name to me -- he is a Marine, just like my Dad.

Love,

Suzy Turner

Peterson, Douglas "Pete" (Ambassador) and Carlotta

EVERSON, DAVID

Name: David Everson
Rank/Branch: O4/U.S. Air Force
Unit: 354 TFS
Date of Birth: 04 September 1931
Home City of Record: Aitkin MN
Date of Loss: 10 March 1967
Country of Loss: North Vietnam
Status (in 1973): Returnee
Aircraft/Vehicle/Ground: F105F #8335
Other Personnel in Incident: Jose Luna, returnee

From: Nancy Kivler
11 Feb 2002

Lt. Col Everson:

You don't know me but tonight (Monday, Feb. 11,2002) while watching the news WTVT channel 13 in Gulfport, FL I saw the piece on the POW bracelets it touched me and I remembered I had a bracelet that I got when I was just a teenager (I'm 46 yrs old now). I went into my room and there in the drawer with all my family pictures was a bracelet with your name on it. I then went to the computer and logged on to the WTVT.com for on local TV station and followed the POW page till I came across your name and your biography. It made me feel very strange that something I received as a teenager actually belongs to someone that is truly a person and not just an unknown name but actually a man who came home to his wife and children it really shook me up and made me think. I just wanted to write this to let you know that I have your bracelet after all these years. I hope all is well with you and your family I know they must be very proud of you, I know I am.

By the way my name is Nancy Jo Kivler I am 46 years old with a husband that I have been married to for 18 years and we have a wonderful 17 year old daughter, I would be very interested in hearing from you and return your bracelet if you would like it, if not I will understand but I will keep the bracelet to remind me of what you did for me and this country.   Thank You So Much...

Nancy Kivler

THOMPSON, WILLIAM JAMES
Rank/Branch: O6/U.S. Air Force
Unit: 399th Tactical Fighter Squadron, Da Nang Air Base, South Vietnam
Date of Birth: 19 February 1933
Home City of Record: Houston TX
Loss Date: 01 August 1968
Status (in 1973): Missing In Action
Category: 3
Acft/Vehicle/Ground: F4D (pilot)

From: Dee Riggs
31 Jan 1999

My bracelet says Maj. William Thompson, 8/1/68, with a blue star.

I have held the POW/MIA bracelet of Maj. Thompson since the beginning. Although I have not worn the bracelet (since I became allergic to it many years ago), this man has been in my heart. Through the technology of the internet, I have learned of Maj. (Col.) Thompson's status. It's strange how I can be here with tears in my eyes caring for someone I never knew, but my heart is so full. Not only of tears, because he hasn't come home yet, but of the sacrifice he has made, I will always be so grateful.

Thanks to him and his family. I will continue to pray for you.

Sincerely,

Dee Riggs

CLAXTON, CHARLES PETER
Remains Identified 10/28/2000

Rank/Branch: O4/U.S. Air Force
Unit: 314th Tactical Airlift Wing, Nha Trang Airbase, South
Vietnam
Date of Birth: 22 December 1932
Home City of Record: Chicago IL
Date of Loss: 29 December 1967
Country of Loss: North Vietnam
Status (in 1973): Missing In Action
Category: 4
Acft/Vehicle/Ground: C130E

From: Marie Witkay
30 Aug 2000

Dear Family:

While I am a stranger to you, I have been praying for you and Maj. Claxton since 1967. You see, in 1967 my then boyfriend, Tony was drafted out of college and was sent to Viet Nam. We did get married before he went and when he returned, as so many other young couples, he came home to a wife and 3 month old baby girl.

It goes without saying that Viet Nam took over my entire life with Tony in the Army. It was at that time that I bought a "POW/MIA silver bracelet" with the name of Major Charles Claxton, 12-29-67 on it. It was just "luck" that I got his name and not someone else'. For these past many, many years I have prayed, worried and wondered what happened to him. Then just yesterday, someone told me I could find this kind of information on the web - which leads me to writing you this letter.

My husband did come home in one piece, we now have two grown children, daughters 32 and 30 years of age. They are married with children of their own - we have 4 grandchildren and another one on the way. Tony and I have been married for going on 34 years. I do not tell you this out of some sense of what I have and you do not. I only say this to somehow tell you how much I can feel, to the best that I can without going through what you have been through, your sorry for your loss. Even though times were very tough and hard when Tony came back, it cannot compare with the void you must still feel.

My father was a lifer in the Marines. I am well acquainted with the "entire picture."

I guess the bottom line that I want you to know is that on August 30, 2000, there is still someone out there who, even though they are a stranger to you and of course Maj. Claxton, his life and sacrifice is NOT FORGOTTEN. I still have his bracelet and look at it quite often. Life is strange. Sometimes, so many times, we are totally unaware how we can impact and possibly change someone's life who we have never met. Maj. Claxton has had an impact on mine.

God bless you all.
With sincere gratitude,

Marie J. Witkay

Leonard, Lt Col Edward USAF (Ret)

MOORE, WILLIAM RAY
Rank/Branch: E5/U.S. Navy
Unit: USS Long Beach
Date of Birth: 21 December 1945
Home City of Record: Princeton KS
Date of Loss: 02 October 1969
Country of Loss: North Vietnam/Over Water
Status (in 1973): Killed/Body Not Recovered
Category: 5
Aircraft/Vehicle/Ground: C2A

From: Sara Morton & QM3 Chadwick D. Morton, USS Mahan, US Navy
3 Sep 2000

Today, I took my son to visit the Moving Wall in Waterford, CT. I have been to the monument in D.C., but I wanted my son to see this because I feel it is so very important. Anyhow, we came home and I have been thinking about it since. My husband is in the US Navy and we have recently been transferred to Norfolk, VA. I am still here in CT packing up. Well, to get my mind off of all this sadness, I decided to work on some packing. I came across my bracelet with the name MM2 William R. Moore. I didn't realize that I had still had it. It was given to me about 13 years ago by my aunt who taught me the importance of the War and what it meant to this country. I decided to check and see if his remains had been found yet, but found that his body has yet to be recovered and where his name is listed on the Wall. During my visit today, I brought flowers in memory of all who died. But I think I will return tomorrow with flowers for him. Today, I renew my commitment to wear his name. When I was given the bracelet, I was only 12 and the novelty of wearing it eventually wore off. But I never abandoned it. I have lived in many places and tend to throw things away before moving. But this bracelet has always remained with me, tucked back in my jewelry box where I found it today. I am glad I found it. It makes the sad visit today mean something. So to the family of William R. Moore, I will never forget and you will always be with me in my heart. We will continue the traditions of the Navy that you kept so many years ago.

Sara Morton & QM3 Chadwick D. Morton, USS Mahan, US Navy

BIVENS, HERNDON ARRINGTON
Rank/Branch: E4/U.S. Army
Unit: Security Platoon, 52nd Aviation Battalion, 17th Aviation
Group, 1st
Aviation Brigade
Date of Birth: 01 January 1951 (Frankfort Germany)
Home City of Record: Jamaica NY
Date of Loss: 15 April 1970
Country of Loss: South Vietnam
Status (in 1973): Missing In Action
Category: 1
Aircraft/Vehicle/Ground: UH1H
Other Personnel in Incident: Roger A. Miller (Released POW)

From: COL. Donald C. Summers
2 Aug 1999

My name is Donald C. Summers. On 15 April 1970 I was a SP5
assigned to the 170th Assault Helicopter Company. Our helicopter
was shot down at LZ Orange over looking Dak Seang SF Camp,
and we spent 10 hours on the hill surrounded by an NVA
Division. My pilot Al Barthelme died on the hill, the copilot WO
Roger Miller was taken prisoner and was returned in operation
Homecoming in 1973. A pathfinder, CPL Herndon A. Bivens was
reported killed by WO Miller when the two were taken prisoner
the day after the crash. Basically this is all the information I have
on Bivens. I am wanting to find out who he was, where he was
from and what if any awards he may have received for that action.
He was a very brave man to whom I owe my life.

COL. Donald C. Summers
USA, SF, Retired

BEDINGER, HENRY JAMES
Rank/Branch: O2/U.S. Navy
Unit: Fighter Squadron 143, USS Constellation (CVA 64), pilot
Date of Birth: 30 March 1945 (Philadelphia PA)
Home City of Record: Hatboro PA
Date of Loss: 22 November 1969
Country of Loss: Laos
Status (in 1973): Released POW
Aircraft/Vehicle/Ground: F4J
Missions: 30
Other Personnel in Incident: Herbert Wheeler, pilot

From Geri McElroy
16 Dec 2001

...As soon as I scanned your list, a name jumped out at me. However, I did not want to be swayed without delving a bit deeper, and went through the list one by one, eliminating names by virtue of date of capture (after I started wearing my bracelet); or date of return (before I started wearing my bracelet); or gender, or if a civilian.

My bracelet was engraved with the name of now-retired Commander Henry Bedinger. His date of capture -- 11/22/69 --- had struck me hard when I received my bracelet as it was an anniversary date of President Kennedy's assassination. Although the bracelet is long gone, I can still remember the feel it on my wrist, and remember putting nail polish on the back so my arm would stop turning green from the copper.

Most of all, I remember my joy when I read Lt. Bedinger was safely returned home. So although my memory of the specifics may have faded, I had my own peace of mind.

I read in Commander Bedinger's bio that he served at the Pentagon, and although she was too young to be there when he was, there was a very special young lady, a Navy civilian, who served the Joint Chiefs of Staff proudly, and paid the ultimate price on September 11th. I will not forget Henry Bedinger's name again, for he represents not only what our country endured in the past, but may again in the coming future. And I will not forget the young lady Angie Houtz, beloved daughter of dear friends.

Thank you for all you do, and keep fighting the good fight.

Follow-up 07/12/2002

Perhaps you are aware that Commander Bedinger took the time to contact me via e-mail after reviewing a letter I had sent to you. For so many years I had been haunted by my fuzzy memory of the name on my bracelet, berating myself for forgetting. But I always remembered the last name began with a "B" and was half-convinced the first name began with a "J." When your list was sent to me, I felt strongly it was Commander Bedinger, but his given name of "Henry" threw me. I was thrilled when he wrote back and signed it "Jim." All doubts dissolved.

His letter to me was like a voice from the past, present and future. So any images came flooding back. Being ostracized in high school as a "hawk" when I thought I was just being verbally supportive of Americans away from home, fighting as their country told them to. (for 13 months, from 11/67 to 12/68, I wrote daily to a young Marine in Da Nang, someone I did not meet until his tour ended and he drove from South Carolina to N.Y. in his new 1969 Camaro, just to say hello). Debates seemed a way of life, as did differences of opinions, as did high emotions. Those times were volatile, to be sure, and feelings on Vietnam could make or break relationships, whether old or new.

Commander Bedinger was captured the first semester of my Freshman year in college, and released the last semester of my Senior year. Time spent very differently, to be sure.

I remember that the Marine I wrote to had been advised to wear civilian clothes home, and I was embarrassed for him, and for the tension that had caused that directive. I promised myself I would not allow myself to be ashamed or to hide my feelings again. When the Gulf war broke out, I immediately put yellow ribbons on my mailbox, and stared down anyone that may have questioned it. I do not follow my government blindly, and I think for myself, but I have never been ashamed to express love or thankfulness for my country. Of course, after 9/11, not many questioned flags, or expressions of loyalty. However, more and more, I see such items on sale or clearance at our stores, the rush to have them perhaps waning.

So, we continue to need you, to remind all of what was, what is, and what may be again. War, capture, protests. As I said, Commander Bedinger's email was like a voice from the past, present and future. He was also kind enough to invoke Angie Houtz' name, killed at the Pentagon, just 5 days into turning 27 years old. Perhaps you will remember her also in passing thoughts.

Respectfully,

Geri Gannatti McElroy

Camerota, Joy (Camerota, Maj. Peter USAF (Ret))

Right to Left: Kobashigawa, Tom; Parsels, Maj John; Tabb, MSgt Robert; Elliot, Col Artice; Alwine, Msgt. David; Anshus, Lt Col Richard; Malo, Issako; Prather, CW4 Phillip; Lenker, Michael; Caviani, SGM Jon; Mott, Col David

And They Have Names

By people, I do not mean "personnel."
I do not mean "end strength."
I do not mean "percent of fill" or any of those other labels
which refer to people as a commodity.
I mean living, breathing, serving human beings.
They have needs, and interests and desires.
They have spirit and will, and strengths and abilities.
They have weaknesses and faults.
And they have names.

General Creighton Abrams

LEE, LEONARD MURRAY
Remains Identified 07/27/00

Rank/Branch: O4/U.S. Navy
Unit: Fighter Squadron 114, USS Kitty Hawk (CVA 63)
Date of Birth: 08 July 1935
Home City of Record: Pulaski VA
Date of Loss: 27 December 1967
Country of Loss: North Vietnam
Status (in 1973): Missing In Action
Category: 3
Acft/Vehicle/Ground: F4B

INNES, ROGER BURNS
Remains Returned I.D. Announced 08/29/00

Rank/Branch: O2/U.S. Navy
Unit: Fighter Squadron 114, USS Kitty Hawk (CVA 63)
Date of Birth: 23 March 1943
Home City of Record: Chicago IL
Date of Loss: 27 December 1967
Country of Loss: North Vietnam
Status (in 1973): Missing In Action
Category: 3
Acft/Vehicle/Ground: F4B

From: Cricket Kim
23 Sep 2000

Back when the bracelets were first being made, my two sisters and I each ordered one. That was more than 20 years ago. Since I had an allergy to metals, I was unable to wear my bracelet for long, but I kept it through the years, often wondering if "my guy" ever got home. About 4 years ago, I lost the bracelet but never forgot about Leonard. I often wondered if I could get another bracelet with his name, but never got around to it. recently my younger sent me an e-mail link to your site and was dismayed to learn that Leonard was still missing.

I also found out that his "backseater" Roger Innes was also still missing. This revelation was somewhat disturbing to me. Many times through the years I had wondered about Leonard's family, if he had a wife and children, if his parents were still alive, how they had coped through the years with the uncertainty of his fate. They had been in my prayers many times.

Last month I was in DC and went to the Wall and found Leonard's name. It was heartrending, to say the least. I had looked through several vendor's boxes of bracelets and not found his name among them. After looking through the last vendor's boxes twice, I told him how I had lost mine and inquired if there was a way I could request a specific name. He asked if I had looked through the "white ones, they're Navy". I had, but I looked again just to appease him. Much to my surprise and joy there he was, no longer a LtCdr now a Cdr!!!!
My husband could not understand the emotions running through me at that moment as I stood there with tears running down my cheeks. He wanted to try to comfort me, but since he hadn't lived with this most of his life, he could not understand, and I could not explain.

Last week there was a small article in our local paper that two Navy aviators had been identified and were to be returned to their families for burial. They identified Roger Innes, but the family had requested that the second man's identity not be revealed. Thanks to this site, I had become aware of the connection of Roger Innes and Leonard Lee, and knew that he had finally come home. I was numb as I read the article, and prayed for his family. I was a mass of differing emotions - relieved that he had not suffered at the hands of the Viet Cong, sad that he was dead, glad he had been found, anxious for his family.

My new bracelet will someday be handed down to my grandson. He will be told of the ultimate price Leonard Lee and all the others paid for us.

I hope that Leonard's family sees this someday and knows that he will never be forgotten.

Cricket

POOL, JERRY LYNN
Rank/Branch: O2/U.S. Army Special Forces
Unit: SOA (MACV-SOG), CCN, 5th Special Forces
Date of Birth: 02 April 1944 (Sinton TX)
Home City of Record: Freeport IL
Date of Loss: 24 March 1970
Country of Loss: Cambodia
Status (in 1973): Missing In Action
Category: 3
Acft/Venicle/Ground: UH1H

"(Jerry) Pool's remains were not individually identified, but he has been dentified as art of the group," Greer said. "He is now accounted for so he comes off of our list of MIA soldiers)."   July 1, 2001 The Journal Standard

"I don't think I will be going because it's false. I'm a person who hates lies ... I'll fight for my husband until the day I die. He deserves the truth."   Darlene Pool

From: Gary S. Turk
Date: Fri, 05 Feb 1999 15:54:26 -0700

I obtained my POW/MIA bracelet in 1971. I entered the Army myself in 1972. There was a daily ritual at morning formation, where the Drill Sergeant would yell out and ask if I was wearing that bracelet again. I would reply that yes I was, and would be ordered to remove it. I refused each morning, and as a result would do 50 pushups. The bracelet would go into my pocket for a few hours, and then back on my wrist. I wore this bracelet daily while I was in the service, until 1980. Upon leaving the service, I continued to wear the bracelet.

I hung the bracelet on my wall of memories in my den about 17 years ago. I would see other people wearing their bracelets still, and it would remind me that Jerry Pool was not to be forgotten. I haven't forgotten his name since the first day I wore that bracelet. I often thought about contacting his family, but didn't want to stir up the emotions that might cause. I have also wanted to take it to the Wall, or to a traveling replica that has been here in Colorado a few times. I just can't make myself go. I feel a lot of survivor's guilt, and have a bad time with that. Veteran's Day is real hard for me too. I'm sick that the schools don't even recognize it anymore.

I would like nothing more than to give this bracelet to one of Jerry's family members. I don't know if that would even be appropriate. It may be something too hard for them to do, I really don't know. If nothing else, I would like them to know that I still think about him. I put the bracelet back on, and found the biography concerning Jerry. If people ask me about it, I will be able to tell them about him and his crew. I am a proud veteran, and am proud of the job Jerry Pool did in service to his country.

Gary S. Turk

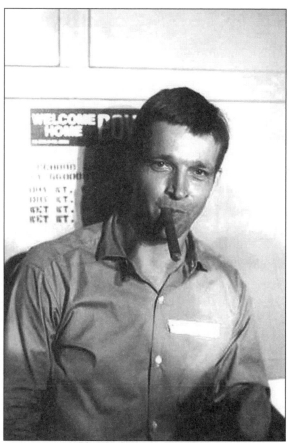

Rice, Cmdr Charles, USN (Ret)

DAVIS, EDGAR FELTON

Rank/Branch: O3/U.S. Air Force
Unit: 11th Tactical Reconnaissance Squadron, Udorn Airfield, Thailand
Date of Birth: 15 December 1935
Home City of Record: Goldsboro NC
Date of Loss: 17 September 1968
Country of Loss: Laos
Status (in 1973): Missing In Action
Category: 2
Aircraft/Vehicle/Ground: RF4C

From: Davis, Philip C4C CS12
16 Nov 2000

Dear Family Members of Capt. Edgar F. Davis,

I am a fourth classman (freshman) at the United States Air Force Academy. I wear the bracelet of Capt. Edgar F. Davis, missing 9-17-68 in Laos, on my wrist. Last week I attended a briefing with another Vietnam era POW. His story moved me, and made me think of Capt. Davis. I do not know where he is today, or what happened to him, but I am eternally grateful for the sacrifice he made.

As a future Air Force officer, I hope that I can uphold the same standards of courage found in those pilots who flew over Laos, Cambodia, and Vietnam. They gave their all when asked, and have gone unnoticed by many. The commitment of Capt. Davis, and others like him, is not lost on me. The story of Capt. Davis will stay with me, and remind me of the heritage I must uphold, and the example I have to follow.

I hope that you will accept my deepest thanks on behalf of Capt. Davis, and know that he is not forgotten. With the utmost respect and gratefulness,

Cadet Fourth Class Philip (P.J.) Davis,
United States Air Force Academy, Class of 2004

HALL, GEORGE ROBERT

Rank/Branch: O3/U.S. Air Force, pilot
Unit: 15th TRS
Date of Birth: 18 June 1930
Home City of Record: Hattiesburg MS
Date of Loss: 27 September 1965
Country of Loss: North Vietnam
Status (in 1973): Returnee
Aircraft/Vehicle/Ground: RF101
Missions: 196

From: Annie B
26 Sep 2001

For many years I wore the POW bracelet of George Robert Hall, USAF. I was a Navy wife living at NAS Miramar and NAS Lemoore, California, and continued wearing the bracelet when we left the Navy and went to Detroit, Michigan.

My oldest daughter, Bonnie Ann, named after an aircraft carrier (Bon Homme Richard), took my bracelet to show and tell at school in the early 70's (and lost it). I watched the for Hall's name when our returnees came home, but never saw it.

Now I live near NAS Pensacola, Florida and visited The Wall South and was relieved to not find George Robert Hall's name. Yet, I always wondered what happened to him. Today I was searching the internet to find remembrance bracelets for those who lives were taken on September 11, 2001 and happened upon this website. Lo and behold I found the name of George Robert Hall and discovered he was released in 1973.

When I visit the Vietnam portion of the Naval Aviation Museum at Naval Air Station Pensacola, I wished I would have been able to donate it to their collection of bracelets; since it was lost, I cannot. To this day I always wear my Desert Storm - A Call to Freedom bracelet. It reminds me and others who see it how proud I have been and always will be of our wonderful men and women in the service of their country.

Ann Backhurst

RAY, JAMES MICHAEL
Rank/Branch: E3/U.S. Army
Unit: 525 Military Intelligence Group Team 38
Date of Birth: 10 November 1949 (Cambridge MA)
Home City of Record: Woonsocket RI
Date of Loss: 18 March 1968
Country of Loss: South Vietnam
Status (in 1973): Prisoner of War
Category: 1
Acft/Vehicle/Ground: Ground

From: Denise Gasta
9 Jan 2001

I have been wearing Jimmy's bracelet since late 1987. My husband bought me a gold ID bracelet this past Christmas. He had Jimmy's information engraved on it. He said Jimmy deserved gold, not steel. I agree with him.

Respectfully and hopefully yours,
Denise Gasta

One of the Prison Camps

STUTZ, LEROY WILLIAM
Rank/Branch: O2/U.S. Air Force
Unit: Udorn Airbase, Thailand 11th TRS
Date of Birth: 13 November 1939
Home City of Record: Effingham, KS
Date of Loss: 02 December 1966
Country of Loss: North Vietnam
Status (in 1973): Released POW
Aircraft/Vehicle/Ground: RF4C
Missions: 65

From: Jim McGinnis
16 Apr 2001

My wife and I recently returned from a family trip to Washington DC. After exploring the monuments, my son and daughter had plenty of questions. But even as an American History teacher, I struggled with explaining to my children the gravity of the Vietnam War. My wife and I grew up during the 60's and 70's in this once sleepy Florida town.

Although too young ourselves to fully comprehend things, we were fully aware that brave men were serving our country and some were not coming back. My wife wore a POW bracelet with the name Leroy Stutz. Until recently, we had no idea of how to find you...or whether you wanted to be found. And I suppose that we, like many Americans, were guilty of trying to put Vietnam behind us. I sincerely apologize for the fact that it took us so long to try to contact you. We took the bracelet with us to DC, praying we would not find your name on Wall.

It is important that you know that there were people thinking of you, while you suffered through such a terrible ordeal. It is also important for you to know that the bracelet helped two generations of naïve kids understand the price men paid for our country...

With respect and gratitude,

Jim and Kay McGinnis

JUDD, MICHAEL BARRY
Rank/Branch: E4/U.S.Marine Corps
Unit: A Company, 3rd Reconnaissance Battalion, 3rd Marine Div
Date of Birth: 22 August 1945
Home City of Record: Cleveland OH
Date of Loss: 30 June 1967
Country of Loss: South Vietnam
Status (in 1973): Killed/Body Not Recovered
Category: 3
Aircraft/Vehicle/Ground: CH46A

From: Thomas Teleha
15 Apr 2001

To the family of HM3 Michael Barry Judd,

Since attending Hospital Corps "A" School in January of 1990, I have worn the bracelet bearing his name. I chose his bracelet out a group of bracelets that the Command Master Chief had. It wasn't until August of 1993 that I learned who he was. At that time I was attending the Navy's Cardiovascular Technologist "C" School at National Naval Medical Center in Bethesda, MD. His picture, along with a dozen other Hospital Corpsman, hang on the wall in the corridor of The Naval School of Health Sciences.

A month or so later, my younger sister, who was living south of D.C. at the time, said she would very much like to go into town and visit the Wall. When we arrived, I was overwhelmed at the true size of the memorial. Many emotions came to me that day. At the entrance to the memorial, there is a book listing all of the POW's and their location on the wall. I looked for his name and along with the other information, it told me his birthday. When I read that information, I got chills, August 22, 1945. The same day as mine, August 22, 1967. I was born about two months after he was declared MIA. I still wear his bracelet each and every day, showing my respect and to honor him and all the other vets still over there. I am still on active duty in the Navy, 14 years, and am currently a second class petty officer, hoping to make E-6 soon. I wish all of you the best and hope that he comes home someday. God bless you.

Thomas M. Teleha, HM2(SS/FMF), USN

MILLINER, WILLIAM PATRICK

Rank/Branch: W1/U.S. Army
Unit: Troop B, 7th Squadron, 1st Cavalry, 164th Aviation Group
Date of Birth: 12 June 1950
Home City of Record: Louisville KY
Date of Loss: 06 March 1971
Country of Loss: Laos
Status (in 1973): Missing In Action
Category: 1
Aircraft/Vehicle/Ground: AH1G

From: Karen Weaver
17 Jun 2001

To the Family of WO1 William Milliner

My name is Karen Weaver. I am wearing a POW/MIA bracelet with your son's name. I have been wearing this bracelet since 1971. I feel that he also belongs to me since he had been part of my life for the last 30 years.

Recently I went to Washington on a field trip with my son's school. After all this time I finally got the courage to go to the Wall. It was one of the most profound experiences of my life. All of the children on the bus looked for his name when we arrived and he became real and part of their lives for a little while too. They also learned what it means to keep a promise as I have done these last 30 years.

I have never taken this bracelet off! I promised 'till they come home and that is exactly what I have done.

Karen

HASTINGS, STEVEN MORRIS
Rank/Branch: E5/U.S. Army
Unit: 240th Assault Helicopter Co, 214th Aviation Btn., 12th
Aviation Group
Date of Birth: 11 October 1948
Home City of Record: Baldwin Park CA
Date of Loss: 01 August 1968
Country of Loss: South Vietnam
Status (in 1973): Missing In Action
Category: 4
Aircraft/Vehicle/Ground: UH1C

From: Samuel S. Knudsen
21 Feb 1999

To the Family and Friends of Sgt. Steven M Hastings,
    I have, for so many years, had Sgt. Steven Hasting's bracelet. It was given to me by an elderly woman that was nearing death and feared it would be discarded upon her death. She gave it to me. She must have known I would care; that I would keep caring. Although I discussed it as often as appropriate, I could not find the strength to wear it. I was afraid I would lose faith. The bracelet has sat out on my dresser for the past few years. Recent events, added years, and maturity, have made me more aware, more in touch with my own feelings regarding life and family; the lives of service men/women, my father among them. Perhaps it is my own mortality or witnessing my child grow that gives me this new sense of being. It is with the power of the internet, that I write.
    I sorry for Steven's sake that I didn't have the guts to wear it.
    I am sorry for my father's sake that I have not been more vocal, more demanding of my government.
    I hope you all have had the strength I have lacked.
    I pray that your lives have been filled with love and hope.
    I pray that others find a new sense of compassion, understanding, and tolerance for the fellow human beings as I have.

I pray that we as a people can hold tight to are faiths (in all things).

I pray nothing I have done or said offends you in any way. I pray for you all, God's blessings.

Respectfully,

Samuel S. Knudsen

POWs await their turn for formal transfer to U.S. custody

STRATTON, CHARLES WAYNE

Rank/Branch: O3/U.S. Air Force
Unit: 34th Tactical Fighter Squadron, Korat Airbase, Thailand
Date of Birth: 09 October 1940
Home City of Record: Dallas TX
Date of Loss: 03 January 1971
Country of Loss: Laos
Status (in 1973): Missing in Action
Category: 2
Aircraft/Vehicle/Ground: F4

From: Laurie Weckstein
29 May 2001

On this Memorial Day, my thoughts rest with the man whose name was on my bracelet I first wore as a 12 year old. I am now 40. These 28 years later, I haven't forgotten you and what your life meant to our country.

I never really knew what happened to you. From what I can find, you remain, listed as an MIA, in Laos. Still, I remember your name and the sacrifice you made so that I can sit here today with my beautiful family, my life . . . my freedom.

I thank and honor you Capt. Charles Stratton. Whether you are alive today, or not ... you are remembered. I am profoundly grateful to you, and to all the other men and women who have risked their lives, for upholding honor, democracy and freedom -- in it's purest, most heart-wrenching, selfless form.

To your family and loved ones, I offer this quote by Abraham Lincoln. I hope that perhaps, in some way, these incredible words may help.

" . . . I feel how weak and fruitless must be any words of mine which should attempt to beguile you from the grief of a loss so overwhelming. But I cannot refrain from tendering to you the consolation that may be found in the thanks of the Republic they died to save. I pray that our heavenly Father my assuage the anguish of your bereavement, and leave you only the cherished memory of the loved and lost, and the solemn pride that must be yours to have laid so costly a sacrifice upon the altar of freedom."
Abraham Lincoln ~ November 21, 1864

I will always remember your name and what your life stands for ...

Laurie Galbraith Weckstein

White, Maj. Robert USA (Ret), the last POW released

KEY, WILSON DENVER
Rank/Branch: O3/U.S. Navy
Unit: Attack Squadron 34, USS Intrepid (CVS 11)
Date of Birth: 22 June 1940 (Wilkesboro NC)
Home City of Record: Hayes NC
Date of Loss: 17 November 1967
Country of Loss: North Vietnam
Status (in 1973): Released POW
Aircraft/Vehicle/Ground: A4C
Missions: 90

From: Teri Santagata
14 Sep 2000

In 1972, at the age of 14, I bought a POW/MIA bracelet from a fellow high school student. The name on the bracelet was "Lt. Denver Key" who was listed as a POW/MIA on 11-17-67. During the releases of the POW's, my father and I kept up vigils to see if he returned. Lt. Denver Key was not listed as those returned.

As I made a vow to keep the bracelet on until he returned, either live or identified, I kept the bracelet on. My mother and I had the worst argument on my wedding day as I insisted on wearing it, although it didn't match the rest of my jewelry. I didn't care. I made a promise, one I intended to keep.

For 28 years, I wore this bracelet, and there wasn't a day that went by that I didn't think of Lt. Denver Key. I wondered about him, his whereabouts, his family. The only time I took the bracelet off was when I was giving birth or undergoing an operation. And that was only because the hospital made me! Even then, it was the first thing I asked for when I came out of the fog.

I tried getting in touch with his family. I went to the local VA, only to find that my bracelet was probably a "hoax" bracelet and that he never existed. However, something told me to keep the bracelet on.

On September 12, 2000, I went on line and went to a site a friend sent me. It had to do with birthdays and who was born or had died on that date. I noticed at the bottom of the screen it said something about Vietnam POW/MIA's and the date they were last seen or captured. I entered Lt. Denver Key's date as on my bracelet.....LO AND BEHOLD!!!!!!! He had been released in 1973!

Why he wasn't listed is because he goes by his middle name (Denver) and not his birth first name. I was shocked, to say the least. He was alive??? After all this time thinking he was either dead or a hoax???

I managed to obtain his phone number, and I called his house tonight (9/13). His very sweet and kind wife answered, and I talked to her, telling her why I was calling, etc. He wasn't at home at the time, and I gave her my phone number to call back, if he wanted. And he did.

It was hard to talk to him without crying, but I tried my best. I told him that I would send the bracelet to him, as I think it is up to him as to what should be done with it. I only had the honor of wearing it all these years. I think the most wonderful thing about our conversation was when he said, and I quote "You have my permission to take the bracelet off." To think about this still brings tears to my eyes.

To those of you who still wear the POW/MIA bracelets from years and years ago, and to those who have recently started wearing them, my hat's off to you. I wore mine through thick and thin and don't regret a moment of it. I plan on mailing mine to Lt. Denver Key in order that he can realize that people out here were concerned about his fate while he was imprisoned. However, my wrist feels bare at this time. I think it's time to get a new bracelet.

Teri Santagata

PERRY, THOMAS HEPBURN
Rank/Branch: E4/U.S. Army Special Forces
Unit: Detachment A-105, 5th Special Forces Group
Date of Birth: 19 June 1942 (Washington DC)
Home City of Record: Canton Center CT
Date of Loss: 12 May 1968
Country of Loss: South Vietnam
Status (in 1973): Missing In Action
Category: 2
Aircraft/Vehicle/Ground: Ground

From: Lisa Bailey
17 Jun 2001

In my search for locating family members of Sgt. Thomas Hepburn Perry, I located his niece and learned he has one son, Tommy. His wife never remarried. I would love to send out a very special and loving Father's Day wish for this wonderful man who served his country and was lost in South Vietnam on May 10, 1968.

I received a POW bracelet with his name on it when I was 10 years old. I am now grown, 37, and have a family of my own. I still wear this bracelet with pride and love for a man I do not know.

May God bless him and his family today on Father's Day, 2001.

Lisa Bailey

ROBERTSON, JOHN LEIGHTON
Rank/Branch: O4/U.S. Air Force, pilot
Unit: Ubon, Thailand 555th TFS
Date of Birth: 11 October 1930
Home City of Record: Seattle WA
Date of Loss: 16 September 1966
Country of Loss: North Vietnam
Status (in 1973): Missing In Action
Category: 2
Acft/Vehicle/Ground: F4C

From: Dave
29 May 2001

To the family of Col. John Robertson of Seattle, Washington, shot down September 16, 1966.

I am a Television news anchor who has been wearing Col. Robertson's bracelet everyday since 1971. This is the 30th year I have worn it. I am former active Army during the Vietnam War but did not serve in Vietnam. I wear his bracelet to remind myself that the war that ended for America is still not over for families that have lost a loved one in the Vietnam War. It's also a reminder that our freedoms are won by the heroic efforts of people like John Robertson. I would like to know more about him since I am frequently asked about him as people inquire about my POW/MIA bracelet.

Sincerely,

"Dave"

MCGAR, BRIAN KENT
Remains returned 02/97

Rank/Branch: E3/U.S. Army
Unit: LLRP, 3rd Brigade, 25th Infantry Division
Date of Birth: 17 August 1947 (Turlock CA)
Home City of Record: Ceres CA
Loss Date: 31 May 1967
Country of Loss: South Vietnam
Status (in 1973): Missing in Action
Category: 2
Acft/Vehicle/Ground: Ground

From: Mark A. Rehl
12 Jul 2001

This is to the family of PFC Brian Kent McGar 5/31/67.

I have been wearing Brian's POW bracelet for the last 31 years, never taking it off. EVER! NOT FOR ANYTHING!

I was doing some research for Veteran's issues and came across the POW NETWORK site and checked it out. I have a friend who was a POW for 5 1/2 years and decided to check his name out. I read all of the info on him and then decided to check out Brain's info. I was absolutely stunned to find out that Brain came home over 4 years ago. I had no idea that this had happened. The ironic thing is that I am currently President of Vietnam Veterans Of America Chapter 55 in Licking County, Ohio.

Brian has been my constant companion for over 31 years and I am in a true quandary as to whether or not to continue to wear his name on my wrist. I want to continue to honor Brian and all of the rest of my "Brothers In Arms".

As I tell all of the school children at the classes that we V.V.A. members teach - "I do not wear this bracelet to call attention to myself - I wear it to honor those who gave the supreme sacrifice AND to remind myself as to how very lucky my family has been through World War II, Korea and Vietnam". No member of the Rehl family has died in conflict since the Civil War.

I just wanted to let you know how proud I have been to have worn Brian on my strong right arm all these many years. He wasn't heavy - he is my brother.

Writing this letter has given me the answer to my question as to whether or not to continue wearing Brian's name.

Yes - I am going to continue doing so. I feel that Brian would want it for our brothers who have not come home.

Thank you for Brian, my brother.

Mark A. Rehl
President
Vietnam Veterans Of America,
Chapter 55
Licking County, Ohio

Drabic, Peter; Long, Julius Jr.; Baird, William; Kerns, Gail

BALDOCK, FREDERICK CHARLES JR.
Rank/Branch: O2/U.S. Navy
Unit: VA 94
Date of Birth: 10 May 1939
Home City of Record: Pittsburgh PA
Date of Loss: 17 March 1966
Country of Loss: North Vietnam
Status (in 1973): Released POW
Aircraft/vehicle/Ground: A4C
Missions: 80+

From: Gene Chalin
16 Mar 2000

I have been wearing a POW/MIA bracelet with the name F. Charles Baldock on it since 1972. When ever anyone asks me about the bracelet, I gladly tell them what I thought it stood for, why I still wear it, and everything I thought I knew about the man who is named on it. The one I wear now is actually a second one. I ordered it after the original broke around 1990. I do still have the original in a box my wife keeps of things to pass on to my sons. She understood that was only if Mr. Baldock were never found. In the early years, I often thought of seeing his name in the news as just found or released and then giving the bracelet to him in person. As more and more time passed, the prospects of this "fantasy" coming to life dwindled. I would do some kind of search every few years to see if I could get information on and find "my" MIA. I did so when I ordered my current bracelet in 1990 from The League of American Families. At that time they told me he was still listed as POW/MIA. I was shocked, and overwhelmed with relief and joy, when I saw the listing and bio showing he was released in 1973.

I cannot begin to express the joy, elation, et al I felt when I saw the name listed as released. I have prayed so many times over the past 28 years, that he was still alive some where. Not still a captive, but maybe living in some obscure place, having fallen through the bureaucratic cracks when released and not reported as such. Every Memorial Day and Veterans Day, I always make sure I do something to remember and honor him.

I am glad the "obscure" place turned out to be main stream America. And to finish his career in the Navy! To see the positive attitude he came out of his experience with gladdens my heart immensely. I have seen many [friends and acquaintances] return home from similar circumstances and go into an almost inescapable despair.

I am often asked why do I still wear the bracelet. I simply say, I said I would wear it until he [Mr. Baldock] comes home, and he hasn't yet. Well, I am EXTREMELY glad to find out that not only can I now take it off, but I could have done so 27 years ago!!

I would still like to give him the bracelets.

Thank you Mr. Baldock for the sacrifices you made for this country of ours. It is because of the sacrifices made by you and many thousands like you that this remains the greatest nation on this planet.

Gene

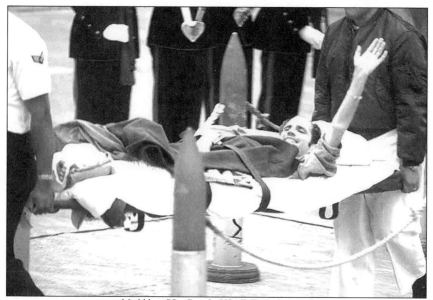

Maddden, SSgt Roy Jr USAF (Ret), deceased

BROWNING, RALPH THOMAS

Rank/Branch: O2/ U.S. Air Force
Unit: 333 TFS
Date of Birth: 25 October 1941
Home City of Record: Orlando FL
Date of Loss: 08 July 66
Country of Loss: North Vietnam
Status (in 1973): Returnee -- Originally listed as Killed In Action
Aircraft/Vehicle/Ground: F105 # 0158

From: Kim Cunningham
2 Aug 2001

Dear Mr. Browning,

I was in JR High school when I purchased a POW bracelet with your name on it. I wore it everyday. I can remember when many of the POWs were being released and I watched them come off of the airplanes one by one on television. I did not see you return and never heard if you made it back. I cried and cried as the men came home and reunited with their families. I tried to find out your status but, prior to the internet, there were very few ways to track down the information. Eventually, my bracelet went in my jewelry box and stayed there for over 25 years. For some reason, each ime I cleaned my jewelry box, I kept it.

I made up my mind to finally find out what happened to you and was surprised how easy it was to read that you were released. I thought it would be a nice gesture to return the bracelet to you and your family...until I found out that many bracelets were produced for the same POW. I thought all along I had the only one with your name. I am sure you have all of the bracelets you would ever want. Unless I hear differently from you, I will keep the bracelet along with a printed copy your story. I am about 25 years or so too late, but I will say it anyway....WELCOME HOME and THANK YOU for what you sacrificed for me, my family, my friends and our country.

Kim Cunningham

MC MILLON JACKIE

MILITARY SERVICE	ARMY
COUNTRY OF CASUALTY	SOUTH VIETNAM
TYPE OF CASUALTY	HOSTILE KILLED
CASUALTY DATE	11/12/65
HOME OF RECORD	CYCLONE, W VIRGINIA
DATE OF BIRTH	02/09/45

From: William Philpot, Jr.
Date: Mon, 5 Apr 1999 01:39:47 EDT

For a High School Friend

To the family of Jackie McMillon,

I saw Jackie daily for the four year period of high school until we graduated in 1963. I knew him as a friend, and I now regard him with the highest esteem that I can give - a boy yet a man.

I feel much love for Jackie.

He gave his life so that we would have a more prosperous country and we could live in a country free from communism and aggression,

Deepest love,

William Philpot, Jr.

ALLARD, RICHARD MICHAEL

Rank/Branch: SP4/U.S. Army
Unit: 119th Aviation Company, 52nd Aviation Battalion, 17th Aviation Group, 1st Aviation Brigade
Date of Birth: 24 August 1946 (Bay City MI)
Home City of Record: Chesaning MI
Date of Loss: 24 August 1967
Country of Loss: South Vietnam
Status (in 1973): Missing In Action
Category: 4
Acft/Vehicle/Ground: UH1H

From: Jimmy Osterman
6 Sep 2001

Allard family;

I have had Richard's bracelet for almost 30 years. I was with the 25th. Div. assigned to the 2/27 Wolfhounds.

I did not know Richard was from Saginaw County till a few years ago. I have been attempting to contact the family for three years. I have asked every one I know and all they say is his father may have been a doctor.

I have not removed his bracelet and will until......... One more thing, I live in Saginaw and did not know Richard was from the area.

Follow-up: You gave me information on Mrs. Allard. I called her today and talked for an hour. Come to find out her other son was also in the same area as her son that was shot down.

Then we find out so was I.

Jim Osterman

Ragland, Dayton – MIA/PFOD, POW Returnee Korea, top left; Handrahan, Eugene – MIA/PFOD, top right; Milliner, Patrick –MIA/PFOD, bottom left; Rowe, James "Nick" (escapee/assassinated).

SHRIVER, JERRY MICHAEL

Name: Jerry Michael "Mad Dog" Shriver
Rank/Branch: E7/U.S. Army Special Forces
Unit: CCS - MACV-SOG, 5th Special Forces
Date of Birth: 24 September 1941 (De Funiak Springs FL)
Home City of Record: Sacramento CA
Date of Loss: 24 April 1969
Country of Loss: Cambodia (some older records say Laos)
Status (in 1973): Missing In Action
Category: 4
Aircraft/Vehicle/Ground: Ground

From: Ken Lane
Date: Mon, 04 Jun 2001 20:51:30 -0700

This is about the thoughts I have every day for Jerry Shriver. When I wake up every morning, my eyes are drawn to the Band of stainless steel that encircles my right wrist, and I wonder what your eyes are drawn to every morning. When I get up, I can feel where the bracelet has crimped down, pinching me, and I wonder about the discomfort that you must feel after 32 long years. On the 24th of April, I wonder about the desperation that you must have felt when you realized that you and your Yards were trapped with no way out. And I can't help but wonder how you must have felt as the days passed and nobody came to rescue you.

My God, Jerry, I'm sorry. I wish that there was something that could be done. My thoughts and Prayers are with you every single day. I'll wear that bracelet until my death or your return. It's the least I can do after all that you've done.

Ken Lane

ARNOLD, WILLIAM TAMM
Rank/Branch: O2/U.S. Navy
Unit: Attack Squadron 22, USS Coral Sea (CVA 43)
Date of Birth: 25 June 1940 (Milwaukee WI)
Home City of Record: West Allis WI
Date of Loss: 18 November 1966
Country of Loss: North Vietnam/Over Water
Status (in 1973): Missing in Action
Category: 2
Aircraft/Vehicle/Ground: A4C

From: Trina
6 Dec 2001

To those who loved him most:

In August of this year, I had the honor of singing the National Anthem when the Visiting Wall came to Indiana. My husband and I have a lot of friends who served in Vietnam and we watch them day by day struggling to still cope with the horrors they endured. I have been wearing William's name on my wrist for over a year and when I went to the wall, I went and paid a visit. I was not expecting to get so upset and angry when I saw his name up there, but I did. The only thing I could say to him was your name should not be there until we know for sure if you are gone. In America, you can't prosecute someone for murder unless there is a body, but they say his dead. Yet, there he was.

There isn't a day that goes by that I don't think of him and you. I pray somehow you have been able to find peace. I pray that somehow, soon, we will find out the truth in order that all of those who care for him and all of the others that did not come home, can have closure and know all is well and he is home.

Until then, this bracelet will not come off. If it breaks, I'll get a new one with his name. Please know that there is a woman in Indiana who has been touched by your loved one's life, even though he isn't here. I will be praying for you and William at this time of the year. Others might have forgot, but I never will.

Trina

BROWN, WILLIAM THEODORE

Rank/Branch: E6/U.S. Army Special Forces
Unit: SOA, Command & Control North, (MACV-SOG), 5th
Special Forces Group
Date of Birth: 20 February 1945 (Chicago IL)
Home City of Record: La Habra CA
Date of Loss: 03 November 1969
Country of Loss: Laos
Status (in 1973): Missing In Action
Category: 2
Acft/Vehicle/Ground: Ground

From: Von A Ehman
11 Apr 1999

Family and Friends of William T. Brown,

I have a copper POW/MIA Bracelet with the name S/SS William T. Brown inscribed on it. I purchased the bracelet mail order from the advertising section of Rolling Stone Magazine in 1970. Like many of that generation, I just wanted to be of some help to those caught up in the war.

I wore Bill Brown's POW/MIA bracelet till the end of the Vietnam War. Even though it broke in half several times, I always managed to put it back together with electricians tape so I could continue to wear it. For some reason I just couldn't take it off. It almost became a part of me. In my youth I learned to play the guitar while wearing Bill's bracelet on my left wrist. Looking back I believe wearing Bill's bracelet probably inspired me to be a better musician, especially one on an emotional level. The Vietnam War touched a lot of people, in a lot of ways and hopefully some were positive.

I had always wondered of Bill Brown's fate and have thought of him often over the last 29 years. I got a computer this year and I wanted to find out what I could about the man's bracelet that I had worn. From what I read in his POW Network bio, Bill Brown is a good man. Bill reminds me of my own Father, he also loved people from all walks of life and he enjoyed working with them. My Dad was in the Navy in WW II. I found it coincidental that Bill Brown had two Brothers, I have two Brothers, my Dad had two Brothers and so it went all the way down our family line.

I was very bothered by the war and how our people were treated and I still am.

I hope and pray for Bill Brown and his Family that someday something will be known.

God Bless America.

Von Ehman

Returnee Unknown

HOLMES, DAVID HUGH

Rank/Branch: O3/U.S. Air Force
Date of Birth: 26 March 1938
Home City of Record: Belmont MA
Loss Date: 15 March 1966
Country of Loss: Laos
Status (in 1973): Missing In Action
Category: 2
Acft/Vehicle/Ground: O1E Cessna

From: J. Stewart Constance
12 Sep 2001

To the family of Maj. David Hugh Holmes, USAF:

I am 52 years old now. I remember coming home at Christmas time in 1966 to find 8 high school classmates had died in Nam. I still value their sacrifice for me, my wife, and my three daughters. I do not recall exactly how I obtained my bracelet (I got it from a friend who was ordering them), but as my wife says: "when I met you, you wouldn't take it off. Ever!" I haven't been able to wear it because of my profession for years, but we both know it's place of honor.

Yesterday, September 11, 2001, an act of war and a crime was committed against my country w/ a tremendous loss of life. A part of us all died. We will never be the same. I prayed. I went to give blood. I met a 32 year old reservist there and noted his bracelet. We talked. We remembered. He told me about this site. Glued to the TV yesterday, I awoke today and we (my wife and I) both thought of the change in our world that my daughters and their families will see now. WW II , the "Holocaust" and "Nam" are history lessons to them, distinct parts of our childhood and early adulthood to us.

She asked me if I remembered the name on my bracelet. She said, "Holmes." I looked up this web site and felt the need to tell anyone reading this that we have not forgotten what David Holmes did for us. There will be more David Holmes, because we will continue to stand for "Right" and "Goodness" and will help when others will not. We will defend ourselves and the oppressed, and we will have the God given character to separate "righteous indignation" from "revenge" in our pursuit of those who did this to our homeland. We will loose men in strange places to accomplish this. If David Holmes is forgotten, so too will they be. I am copying this letter to those who might hear once more a request to not let that happen, and to those who I think might remember also. It is not just a Ranger creed to not leave a fallen comrade, it is an American creed. We came from all over this world to be here. When we leave our shores to fight for our God given freedoms, and those of others, we are willing to go. Included in that willingness to go is a desire: we want YOU to bring us back (even if only our remains).

God's mercy and gentle hand on us all, and his guidance through the changes we and our leaders face each day. Let us work hard to find and care for those who survived this attack. Let us comfort and reassure those surviving them, and affected by this tragedy in the days to come. Discuss it with your friends and especially your children. Do not let them forget what evil can do and why we stand up for goodness.

And let us not forget any of them: soldier or civilian.
God gave the day.
Live it well.

J. Stewart Constance

Jensen, LtCol Jay USAF (Ret), deceased

HIVNER, JAMES OTIS
Rank/Branch: O3/U.S. Air Force, pilot
Unit: 43rd TFS
Date of Birth: 20 February 1931
Home City of Record: Elizabethtown PA
Date of Loss: 05 October 1965
Country of Loss: North Vietnam
Status (in 1973): Released POW
Aircraft/Vehicle/Ground: F4C
Missions: 35

From: Karen Owings
31 May 2001

I have the original bracelet that I wore during the time James Hivner was a P.O.W. I would like him or his family to have it. I wore it until is release, and a most interesting part of this is that he was reported missing on Oct 5th which is my birthday. I have often thought about how to return the bracelet and hope this reaches you so you can e-mail back so I can send it to you.

We are so thankful that he returned, and for his bravery. I read in the biography that he resides in Texas and retired. Would love to hear from him and just let him know he was thought of daily and prayed for his return. Thank you, and looking forward to being able to send him the bracelet I wore faithfully every day.

God Bless,

Karen Owings

From "Hiv"
04/02/2002

Hi All,

Please excuse this 'generic form letter' approach, but since I'm already behind in answering queries about the flight, I hope this format will do the job. I wrote this as I thought over the events of last week, so it may be a little ragged, disjointed and probably way too long. Hope it's not too boring.

First, the "Freedom Flights" (FF's) were initiated back in 1973, after all the POW's came home to FREEDOM in the USA. Randolph AFB in San Antonio, TX is a training base for "Instructor Pilots" (IP's - those who teach new guys how to fly). The FF's had a dual purpose. Primarily it was a 'welcome back to the cockpit and the USAF' orientation ride. Secondarily, it was a last flight as the pilot of a jet fighter aircraft, for those who would NOT go back onto flight status due to disabilities and/or physical problems. All POW's who were pilots had one thing in common: We took off on what turned out to be our last mission, but never landed. Now we'd have the chance to do both once again. Our 'fini' flight. I was unable to get back on flight status, primarily due to 'blind spots' in my vision, from beriberi, caused by severe malnutrition.

After "Operation Homecoming" our family, like most, was busy trying to get our lives back together and 'catching up' for all the lost time. At the time, 7-1/2 years to me seemed comparable to Rip Van Winkle's famous sleep. In the early years after returning, the FF's were primarily filled with pilots eager to get back into flying once again, as well they should be.

In the early 80's the folks at Randolph AFB contacted me about getting my FF. I was very interested in getting back in a flight suit one more time, but about that time I began having an inner ear problem (a left over from Vietnam) that affected me with periodic sieges of vertigo. (uncontrollable dizziness) This problem continued for many years, even though we explored every medical avenue available, military and civilian. So, FF's were out of the picture for quite a while. Finally found a specialist in Dallas who said he could 'repair' the problem. In 1992 had the operation and have not been dizzy since. After that comment I KNOW what some of you are thinking.

After that I got this crazy idea that I'd wait until I was 70 to get my FF, hoping they would continue to be available, since there were still quite a few pilots who had NOT yet had their flight. My thinking was ... there were older X-POW's than me, but none were 70 when they had their FF - at least to my knowledge.

OK, so now the big plan is set in motion. Myself and a buddy Dave Hatcher are scheduled to get our flights last March. The wheels are in motion and we're (Phyl and me) raring to go. In mid-March we both came down with pneumonia and couldn't shake it for weeks, so I had to 'cancel' a few days before the event. Dave got his flight and everything went well, without us. I had been coordinating with Major Charlie "Lips" Listak who was going to be my IP on the flight. I called him after Dave's FF and asked how it went. He said all went well and he had me on the schedule for next years FF, on March 22, 2002.

One little detail needs to be added before I continue. The f-4C "Phantom II" is/was a twin engine jet fighter-bomber, with a crew of two. I was the Aircraft Commander in the front seat and a really great guy whom I had been flying with for almost a year, Lt. Tom Barrett, was the pilot in the rear seat. (Our less than kind nickname for backseaters was "GIB" - Guy in Back) Of course, they had names for us too. Anyway, Tom had his FF way back in 1974 and then became and IP in the T-38 until retiring and becoming a very successful financial planner. We are still very good friends and stay in contact through email and occasional reunions, etc. He took a few days off from work to be there with us when I finally got my FF.

Tom flew into Dallas/Ft. Worth last Wednesday, March 20th and spent the night here so we could drive to San Antonio early Thursday morning. Phyl and Bonnie drove over to Glen Rose, Texas to pick up Cindy and they drove to S.A., stopping for only a couple of hours at the "Outlet Mall" north of San Antonio.

As Tom and I arrived At RAFB, we were warmly greeted by a 'programmed moving sign' that said, "Randolph welcomes Jim & Phyllis Hivner" followed by, "Colonel James Hivner - Freedom flyer #191." After securing quarters for our 'family' we proceeded to the flight line and were treated like long-lost brothers. We met everyone in the squadron, including my IP, Major "Lips." He was 41, had a beautiful wife, two children and seemed like a mere child himself.

From there I went to the Flight Surgeon's office to get clearance to fly the next day. Most of the health details had been worked out between the 'Doc' and I weeks earlier, via phone. Once I passed this hurdle with 'flying' colors (little humor there) I was escorted to the Egress trainer in the Squadron. This is where you become familiar with the cockpit controls, parachute harness, seat belt/shoulder harness procedures. In a nutshell, you quickly learn how to get out of the aircraft in a hurry, if something bad happens on the ground or even worse, in the air - ejecting. Keep in mind here that the T-38 "Talon" is a twin engine, jet trainer with a crew of two.

I had NEVER flown in a T-38 before, so EVERYTHING was completely different from what I had flown so many years earlier. Allow me one short 'old man brag' here. After the egress people showed me what to do and how, they had me do it on my own, as quickly as I could, while one of them timed me. I guess the adrenaline was flowing as I moved as quickly as I could. It took me 35 seconds. I didn't know if that was good or bad, until he told me most of the 'youngsters' take 30 seconds. I felt much better after that.

Next to 'Personal Equipment' where I was fitted with all the flight gear. Flight suit, boots, G-suit, gloves, helmet, oxygen mask, parachute, etc. The next day all my equipment had "Hiv" on it. Met several of the x-cons (fellow former POW's) who came down for my flight and all the festivities, so we swapped a few war stories and then headed back to the quarters and met Phyl and the girls when they finally arrived. I still had over 18 hours until I get to fly again, but I was ready to go and really excited about it all. We all had dinner at the club, talked for hours and finally turned in for the night. Next morning (Friday, 22 March) up early. Putting on the flight suit and boots seemed just like the good old days. We headed for the flight line and had a simple breakfast provided by the squadron wives. (just coffee for me - I'm already excited) The wives also had a 'grand' spread of food for all of us at the reception AFTER the flight. We all got on buses and arrived at the Base Theater, already packed with people from the base and local area, for a 'Symposium' consisting of short talks by some former POW buddies. Subjects ranged from "The Early Days" (as POW's - a subject I know a lot about), Communication, Escapes, Humor as a POW, Wives in Waiting (by one of the POW wives) and "The Cuban Program" (by Tom Barrett - who was actually in the program for months). Phyl, Cindy, Bonnie, Tom, Lips and I left at the intermission to get ready for the flight. The flight was scheduled, briefed and flown as a 4 ship formation flight. Briefly, the 'flight briefing' was as follows. (only in MUCH more detail of course) We would start engines at 1135 hrs, taxi out to the number one position and be set for an 1145 take off. We took off in 2 two ship elements and joined after take off. Maj. Listak offered me the chance to 'fly' almost immediately after TO, which I accepted 'gladly, but also hesitantly, since I was STILL not familiar with the aircraft. Of course, he was right there if I screwed up, but fortunately that didn't happen.

(A side comment here: At the briefing, since we were going to be in the #3 aircraft, I mentioned to the pilots in #1, #2 & #4 that I hoped the fact that I had NOT flown an aircraft in 37 years would not be a problem to them. I thought they took it well - since they laughed, at least on the outside) We were to fly over the center of the base, where a "Wreath Laying" ceremony would take place adjacent to the large "Missing Man" statue, at exactly 1220 hours where the #3 aircraft (ours) would pull sharply up and out of the formation, symbolizing the man who is 'missing' (KIA, MIA, POW) from the flight as the result of combat. Due to someone's speech running a little long, we received a call to delay our TOT (Time Over Target) 2 minutes, which we did - exactly! We all flew over the 'target' at 1500 feet, doing 400 knots, at 1222 hours and "Lips" made the pull-up, putting 5-1/2 G's (5.5 times normal Gravity) on the aircraft - and our butts. WOW! That was fun.

It had been a long time, but I LOVED it! We leveled out at about 13,000 feet, rolled over on our back and chased the rest of the flight until we eventually rejoined it in the #3 position. To symbolize that many missing men have once again become part of the squadrons, when we rejoined the flight I called the tower and transmitted, "Freedom Three's In" and received the response from tower, "Welcome home sir." We flew around for about 15 more minutes (lots more fun for me) and finally headed for Randolph and landed, 1, 2, 3 and 4, in perfect spacing. I say that because I did NOT land the aircraft.   :) After we touched down the tower called me again, "Congratulations Freedom Flyer 191."   I can't tell you how great I felt by now. As we taxied back to our start engines spots, there was a large crowd waiting to greet us. Lips suggested I let the chute in the seat when I unbuckle everything, rather than climb out with it on. I undid everything and the maintenance people were there to take the helmet, mask, etc. When I climbed down the ladder I was hit with champagne and fire extinguishers shooting water. Glad it was a warm day, because I got fairly well soaked. Two of the champagne 'squirters' were Phyl and Tom. It was really wonderful! Even after I was on the concrete ramp, I was still about 6 inches off the ground, partly from the 'flying' and partly from the excitement of it all. What a fun ride!   I didn't even notice earlier that the Maintenance personnel had painted "Col. James 'Hiv' Hivner" on the canopy rail. A very neat treat for me. Lots of hugs, kisses, handshakes, even a few tears from Phyl and the girls (and maybe me too, unless that was still champagne in my eyes). Lots of pictures, the press and general all around euphoria was the order of the day for the next half hour or so. We then headed back to the sqdn. building for the outstanding reception I mentioned above. I did (eventually) get to take off the wet G-suit and change into a dry flight suit for the rest of the afternoon. I was still too excited and thrilled to eat, but I did have a drink or two. Everyone ate, talked, laughed, joked, and had a ball until we finally left to get ready for the evening affair. Phyl and the girls left for home late Friday afternoon and Tom and I got all 'cleaned up' for the formal "Dining In" Friday night at the O-club. I won't go into detail about that (by now you're saying, "Oh thank you - thank you") except to say it was a fun night. After the speech and excellent dinner, (by now I was REALLY hungry) they showed slides of all the x-POW's in attendance, who had already flown their FF's and ended the event with a short video of my FF #191, put together nicely by the base photo lab personnel.

Afterwards, we all spent another couple of hours reminiscing about the "good" and the "bad" old days. Sometime after midnight, my long and exciting day, that simply 'flew' by, finally caught up with me so I headed back to my room and 'crashed.'

Next morning Tom and I drove back to Plano. We talked all the way to San Antonio and all the way home! Out for dinner Saturday night and took Tom to D/FW airport Sunday noon.

In conclusion, my "Freedom Flight" ranks way up there on my list, as one of the most exciting days of my life. I've always known I missed flying, but I honestly didn't realize just how much until I got back in that cockpit again. I'm still on a 'high' and it's been a week!

GBU, GBA & cul,

Jim

P.S. Each X-PW has wonderful letters rec'd & our bracelet family is as precious to us as answered prayer. It will forever boggle our mind that so many people loved and prayed our POW's home.

Love,

Jim and Phyllis

Chapter 7

The Last Chapter

MORGAN, HERSCHEL SCOTT
Rank/Branch: O3/US Air Force
Unit: 45th TRS
Date of Birth:
Home City of Record: Candler NC
Date of Loss: 03 April 1965
Country of Loss: North Vietnam
Status (in 1973): Released POW
Acft/Vehicle/Ground: RF101
Missions: 122

Date: Tue, 26 Mar 2002

In 1981, when stationed at Bragg, I was involved with some very compartmentalized planning to rescue POWs held in Laos under Vietnam control. It had the blessing of the President. We had privy to radio intercepts, satellite photos, humint*, and much more. The scale mock up was updated weekly. The operation was abruptly ended in early 81**. Based upon what I saw and heard there were people left.

GB
Scotty

* humint - Human Intelligence. **For more on this mission, see U.S. News and World Report, January 1994 and TIME , October 17, 1994 Volume 144, No. 16, THE AMERICANS LEFT BEHIND.

Remains Returned

Includes:
Vietnam Conflict, Mayaguez,
Glomar Java Sea, Bay of Pigs

Some of the identifications have been disputed or rejected (*) by family members. Even when I.D.s are officially rescinded (+), names remain on this list _forever_. Group Burials (~)are noted. Category 5 remains (#) were considered "_UNRECOVERABLE._" Current as of 07/24/02.

Name	Year ID'd	Name	Year ID'd
Abbott. John	74	Behnfeldt. Roger Ernest	87
Abrams. Lewis H.	97	Belcher. Glenn A	97
Adachi. Thomas Yuii~	95	Bell. Holly Gene	89
Adair. Samuel Y. Jr.	74	Bell. Marvin Earl	95
Allard. Michael John	00	Berkson. Joseph M.	72
Allee. Richard K.	97	Bernhardt. Robert E.	73
Allen. Thomas R.	97	Biediger. Larry William	83
Allen. Wayne Clouse	91	Biggs. Earl Roger	90
Alley. Gerald William	89	Billipp. Norman Karl	96
Alley. James Harold	97	Birch. Joel Ray	72
Amesbury. Harry A. Jr.	01	Biscailuz. Robert Lynn	93
Ammon. Glendon Lee	78	Blackburn. Harry Lee Jr.	86
Amos. Thomas H.	99	Blackwood. Gordon Byron	89
Amspacher. William Harry J.	88	Blair. Charles Edward	88
Anderson. Evelyn	72	Blankenship. Charles H.#	97
Anderson. John S.	73	Blassie. Michael J.	98
Anderson. Robert D.	98	Blessing. Lynn	00
Andrews. William Richard	90	Blevins. Lural L.	75
Apodaca. Victor J.*	01	Blood. Henry F.	98
Appleby. Ivan Dale	95	Bloodworth. Donald B.	98
Arroyo-Baez. Gerasimo	85	Bodden. Timothy P.	00
Ashby. Clayborn Willis Jr.	93	Boffman. Allan Brent	90
Asire. Donald Henry	89	Bollinger. Arthur Ray~	95
Atterberry. Edwin Lee	74	Borah. Daniel Vernon Jr.*	97
Avery. Allen J.	97	Boronski. John	01
Ayres. Gerald Francis#	94	Borton. Robert Curtis Jr.*	95
Bader. Arthur Edward Jr.	90	Bosilievac. Michael Joseph	88
Bailey. John E.	99	Bower. Irvin L.	00
Balamoti. Michael Dimitri	95	Bowling. Roy Howard	77
Barnett. Charles Edward	89	Boyd. Walter	00
Barr. John Frederick	89	Boyles. Howard*	73
Barras. Gregory I.	98	Bracey. Lester Jr. [Bracy]	74
Batiste. Jerald T.	84	Branch. James Alvin	93
Bauer. Richard G.	73	Brand. Joseph W.	77
Bebus. Charles James	88	Brandenburg. Dale~	95
Becerra. Rudy M.	01	Brandt. Keith Allan	90
Bednarek. Jonathan Bruce	89	Brett. Robert A.	02
Begley. Burriss Nelson*	93	Bridges. Jerry	01

Brinckmann. Robert Edwin	89	Cobeil. Earl Glenn	74
Brooks. Nicholas George	82	Cogdell. William Keith	94
Brooks. William Leslie~	95	Cole. Legrande Ogden Jr.	89
Brotz. Danny R.	67	Cole. Richard Milton Jr.~	94
Brown. Donald Hubert Jr.	85	Collazo. Raphael Lorenzo	93
Brown. Earl Carlyle	95	Coltman. Willam C.	02
Brown. Joseph O.	98	Comer. Howard B.	01
Buckley. Jimmy Lee	73	Conaway. Gary Lee*	67
Burdett. Edward Burke	74	Condit. Douglas Craig	93
Burgard. Paul E.	68	Condit. William H.	98
Burnham. Mason I.	99	Conklin. Bernard	88
Burns. Frederick John	95	Conley. Eugene O.	02
Burns. John Robert	93	Connell. James Joseph	74
Busch. Jon Thomas*	88	Connolly. Vincent J.	84
Bush. Elbert W.	99	Cook. Dwight William	95
Bush. Robert Edward	88	Cook. Wilmer Paul	89
Butler. James Edward	97	Coons. Chester Lercy	93
Butt. Richard Leigh	86	Copack. Joseph Bernard Jr.	89
Byars. Earnest Ray	93	Copenhaver. Gregory S.	00
Call. John H. III	97	Cordova. Sam Gary	88
Cameron. Kenneth Robbins	74	Cornwell. Leroy Jason III	96
Cameron. Virgil K.	99	Cozart. Robert Gordon Jr.	89
Cannon. Frances Eugene	85	Craddock. Randall James	89
Capling. Elwyn R.	77	Craig. Phillip Charles	86
Cappelli. Charles Edward	89	Crandall. Gregory Stephen	93
Caras. Franklin Angel	87	Crear. Willis C.	01
Carpenter. Nicholas Mallor	90	Cressey. Dennis C.	74
Carpenter. Ramey L.	98	Cressman. Peter Richard~	95
Carrier. Daniel Lewis	89	Crone. Donald E.	01
Carroll. Roger William Jr.	95	Crowley. John E.	00
Carter. James Devrin	95	Cruz. Carlos	95
Cartwright. Billie Jack	94	Rafael Cruz. Raphael (NMN)~	96
Case. Thomas Franklin	86	Cunningham. Carey A.	98
Castillo. Richard	86	Curran. Patrick	01
Castro. Alfonso R.	73	Cuthbert. Bradley G.	91
Cavil. Jack W.	73	Cuthbert. Stephen Howard	90
Chandler. Anthony Gordon	01	Cutrer. Fred C. Jr.	01
Chapman. Peter H.	97	Daffron. Thomas	99
Cheney. Joseph C.	02	Danielson. Mark Giles~	94
Cherry. Allen Sheldon	99	Darcy. Edward J.	0
Chestnut. Joseph Lyons	95	Dardeau. Oscar Moise Jr.	87
Chestnutt. Chambless M.	85	Darr. Charles Edward	88
Chiarello. Vincent Augustu	88	Davis. Brent E.	97
Christian. David Marion*	86	Davis. Charlie Brown Jr.	95
Christianson. Eugene	02	Davis. Daniel Richard	95
Chwan. Michael D.	85	Davis. Donald V.	98
Clapper. Gean P.	00	Davis. Robert Charles	96
Clark. Donald E. Jr.	77	Dawson. Clyde Duane	77
Clark. John Calvin	97	Dawson. Frank Arthur	93
Clark. Phillip Spratt Jr.	88	De Wispelaere. Rexford J.	95
Claxton. Charles P.	00	Dean. Michael Frank	95
Clay. William C. #	97	Deane. William Lawrence	99
Cleary. Peter **	02	Degnan. Jerry L.	01
Clever. Louis J.~	70	Deitsch. Charles Edward	01
Clifton. David P.	84	Dennison. Terry Arden	74
Coakley. William Francis	89	Devers. David R.	69

Diamond. Stephen W.	77	Fortner. Frederick J.	89
Dickens. Delma Ernest	85	Foster. Paul L.	95
Diehl. William C.	74	Foulks. Ralph Eugene Jr.	93
Doby. Herb	77	Franco. Charles S.	67
Dodge. Ronald Wayne	81	Franklin. Charles E.	88
Dodge. Ward K.	74	Frederick. David Addison	90
Donato. Paul Nicholas	93	Frederick. John William	74
Donnelly. Verne George	91	Frederick. William V	90
Dorsey. James V.~	70	Frink. John W.	94
Doughtie. Carl	98	Frits. Orville B.	67
Dove. Jack Paris Sr.	95	Frye. Donald Patrick	82
Doyle. Michael William	85	Fryer. Ben L.	77
Ducat. Bruce Chalmere	77	Fullam. Wayne E.	87
Dudash. John Francis	83	Fuller. James R.+	85
Duffy. John Everett	96	Gabriel. James Jr.	62
Dunlap. William C.	90	Ganley. Richard O.	95
Dunn. Michael E.	99	Ganoe. Berman Jr.	01
Dyczkowski. Robert R.	00	Ganzinotti. Edward L.	84
East. James B.	97	Garcia. Andres "Andy"	00
Eckley. Wayne A.	00	Gardner. John (Jon) G.	00
Edmunds. Robert Clifton Jr.	88	Garside. Frederick Thomas	91
Edwards. Harry J.	85	Gause. Bernard Jr.	00
Edwards. Harry S. Jr.	96	Gilbert. Paul F.~	94
Egger. John C. Jr.	94	Gilmore. La Juan A.	84
Eidsmoe. Norman E.	99	Gittings. Henry M.	84
Elias. Edward K.	72	Goeglein. John Winfred	95
Elkins. Frank Callihan	90	Golberg. Lawrence H.	77
Elliot. Robert M.	99	Gold. Edward Frank	95
Elliott. Robert Thomas	85	Gollahon. Gene R.	02
Emrich. Roger G.	97	Goodrich. Edwin R. Jr.	85
Engelhard. Eric C.	74	Gopp. Thomas Alan	01
Engen. Robert Joseph	91	Goss. Bernard J.	78
Erwin. Donald Edward#	90	Gott. Rodney H.~	70
Espenshied. John L.	89	Gougelmann. Tucker P.E.	77
Estes. Walter O.	77	Govan. Robert A.	02
Evans. James J.	77	Graham. Alan U.	77
Evert. Lawrence G.	02	Graham. James Scott	85
Fanning. Hugh M.+	84	Grainger. Joseph W.	65
Fantle. Samuel	77	Grammer. William M.	67
Feldhaus. John A.	01	Graustein. Robert S.	85
Fellenz. Charles R.	95	Green. Terance C.	84
Fenter. Charles Frederick*	85	Greer. Robert Lee	91
Ferguson. Walter L.	78	Gregory. Robert Raymond	88
Fernan. William	71	Grewell Larry I.	95
Finch. Melvin W.	85	Griffin. James Lloyd	74
Finney. Arthur Thomas	85	Grissett. Edwin R. Jr.	89
Finney. Charles E.	00	Grubb. Wilmer N.	74
Fisher. Donald E.	00	Hackett. James E.	99
Fisher. Donald G.~	95	Hagan. John Robert	96
Fitton. Crosley J.	75	Hagerman. Robert W.	85
Fitts. Richard A.	89	Haifley. Michael E	85
Fitzgerald. Joseph E.	97	Hall. Harley Hubert*	95
Fivelson. Barry F	01	Hall. James S.	88
Flanigan. John N.	97	Hall. James W.	00
Flynn. George E.	74	Halpin. Richard C.	86
Fobair. Roscoe H.	01	Hamilton. John	97
Ford. Randolph Wright	85	Hangen. Welles	93

Hanson. Robert Taft Jr.	89	Jacobson. Ellwood	n/a
Hanson. Stephen P.	00	Jakovac. John A.	97
Hardy. Arthur Hans	83	James. Samuel Larry*	99
Hardy. John C.	68	Jarvis. Timothy	84
Harned. Gary A.	01	Jefferson. James Milton	00
Harris. Cleveland Scott	85	Jenkins. Paul Laverne	95
Harris. Jeffrey L.	97	Jennings. John W. Jr.	84
Harris. Stephen W.~	95	Jensen. George W.	99
Harrison. Larry G.	02	Jesse. William C.	72
Harrison. Robert Heerman~	94	Johns. Vernon Z.	91
Harrold. Patrick K.	97	Johnson. Allen L.	85
Hart. Thomas Trammell III+	85	Johnson. Buford G.	68
Hartman. Richrd Danner	74	Johnson. Edward Harvey	89
Hartney. James C.	89	Johnson. Guy D.	77
Hartzheim. John F.	99	Johnson. William E.	69
Harworth. Elroy E.	86	Jones. George E.#	97
Haselton. John Herbert	74	Jones. William E.	85
Hatley. Joel Clinton~	90	Judge. Darwin Lee	76
Hatton. Wilton N.~	70	Kardell. David Allen	89
Hauer. Leslie J.	77	Karger. Barry Edwin	94
Haukness. Steven A.	75	Karins. Joseph J. Jr.	88
Hayden. Glenn Miller	93	Karst. Carl F.	94
Heggen. Keith R.	74	Kasch. Frederick Morrison	89
Heideman. Thomas Edward	01	Kaster. Leonard L.	01
Hellbach. Harold James	98	Kearns. Joseph T.	88
Heller. Ivan L.	73	Kennedy. Alan G.	73
Henderson. William R.	69	Kennedy. John W.	96
Hensley. Ronnie L.~	95	Kernan. William	n/a
Herrick. Charles	02	Kier. Larry G.	02
Hertz. Gustav G.	01	Killian. Melvin J.	85
Hessom. Robert Charles	94	Kimsey. William A.	01
Higgins. David Jr.	84	King. Michael Eli	90
Higgins. Tyronne	84	Kirby. Bobby Alexander	89
Hockridge. James Alan	77	Kitchens. Perry C.#	77
Hodges. David L.	99	Klenert. William B.	77
Hoff. Sammie Don	89	Klinck. Harrison Hoyt	85
Hoffman. Terry Alan	94	Klinke. Donald Herman~	94
Holdeman. Robert E.	97	Knight. Billy	68
Holt. Robert A.	99	Knight. Henry	00
Hopper. Earl Jr.	02	Knuckey. Thomas William	93
Hopper. Joseph C.	72	Knutson. Richard Arthur	95
Horne. Stanley H.	90	Kolstad. Thomas C.	77
Horskey. Robert M.~	74	Koons. Dale F	90
Hosken. John C.	01	Kott. Stephen J.*	84
Huard. James L.	97	Kravitz. James Stephen	93
Hudgens. Edward Monroe	96	Kroboth. Stanley Nea	85
Huggins. Bobby Gene	97	Kuhlmann. Charles F.	95
Huneycutt. Charles J. Jr.	89	Kulland. Byron K.	94
Hunt. Leon Andrew~	94	Kwortnik. John C.	85
Hunting. Peter M.	65	Labohn. Garry Russel*	89
Hyde. Michael Lewis	91	Lagerwall. Harry R.	85
Innes. Roger B.	00	Lamp. Arnold William Jr.	95
Ireland. Robert Newell~	95	Laney. Billy R.	00
Irwin. Robert Harry	89	Lauterio. Manuel Alonzo	99
Ivan. Andrew Jr.	96	Lavoo. John A.	99
Jackson. William Braxton	82	Lecornec. John Gilbert	85
Jacobs. John C.	67	Lee. Charles Richard	83

Lee. Glenn Hung Nin	94	McKnight. George P.	74
Lee. Leonard M.	0	McLaughlin. Olen B.#	97
Lehnhoff. Edward W.	87	McLeod. Arthur E.	99
Lehrke. Stanley L.~	94	McMahan. Robert Charles	90
Leonor. Leonardo C.	02	McMahon. Charles Jr.	76
Lewellen. Walter Edward	91	McMican. M. D.	88
Lewis. Merrill R. Jr.	89	McNeil. Clarence L.	70
Liles. Robert L. Jr.	85	McOuade. James R.	99
Lim. Edgar S.	84	McRae. David Edward	02
Lindland. Donald Frederick	83	McWhorter. Henry Sterling	86
Lint. Donald M.~	95	Meadows. Eugene Thomas	94
Lockhart. George B.	89	Mearns. Arthur S.	77
Lodge. Robert A.	77	Medaris. Rick E.	73
Loheed. Hubert B.	94	Meder. Paul Oswald	85
Lono. Luther A.	01	Mein. Michael Howard	89
Lopez. Robert	00	Meldahl. Charles	01
Lucas. Larry F.	02	Melton. Todd M.~	95
Luna. Donald	00	Menges. George B.	80
Lundy. Albro	02	Mercer. Jacob E.~	94
Luster. Robert L.*	76	Metz. James Hardin	77
Lynn. Homer M.~	70	Meyer. William M.	85
Lynn. Robert R.	89	Millard. Charles W.	02
MacDonald. George D+	85	Miller. Raymond D.	84
Macko. Charles	00	Minnich. Richard Willis Jr.	85
Madison. William L.	99	Mongilardi. Peter Jr.**	94
Magee. Ralph Wayne	91	Monroe. Vincent Duncan	78
Mahan. Douglas F.	72	Moorberg. Monte Larue	85
Makel. Janie A.	63	Moorman. Frank D.	69
Mallon. Richard J.	89	Moreira. Ralph Angelo Jr.	90
Mamiya. John M.	88	Morgan. Charles E.	90
Manfrida. Jerry L.	84	Morgan. Charles V.	72
Manning. Ronald J.	00	Morgan. Thomas R.	97
Mape. John C.	99	Morley. Charles	99
Marchand. Wayne Ellsworth	68	Morrill. David Whittier	01
Martin. Aubrey G.	74	Morrill. Merwin Lamphrey	83
Martin. Douglas	99	Morris. Robert J. Jr.	77
Martin. James Edward	93	Morrow. Richard D.	78
Martin. Larry E.	89	Moser. David L.	69
Mateiov. Joseph A.~	95	Murdock. Michael G.	74
Matteson. Glenn (NMN)	91	Murray. Patrick Peter	86
Matthes. Peter R.*	95	Musselman. Stephen O.	81
Maxwell. Samuel C.	89	Nahan. John B.	01
May. David	99	Nelson. David Lindford*~	90
McCain. Marvin R.	73	Nelson. Richard C.	84
McCarty. James L.	97	Nelson. William H.	77
McCleary. George Cariton	91	Ness. Patrick Lawrence	86
McCormick. John Vern	88	Netherland. Roger M.	00
McCrary. Jack	00	Newman. Larry J.	94
McCurry. Robert M.	84	Newsom. Benjamin B.	74
McGar. Brian K.	97	Niggle. Harry T.	70
McGrane. Donald Paul	82	Nyhof. Richard E.~	94
McGrath. James P.	01	Odom. Chester	00
McGrath. William Darrel	85	O'Donnell. Michael	01
McIver. Alexander	72	Offutt. Gary	97
McKenney. Kenneth D.	99	Olaughlin. Stephen M.	73
McKinney. Clemie	88	Olds. Ernest Arthur	96
McKinney. Neil Bernard*	96	Olson. Robert E.~	70

Oneil. John J.	69	Rawlings. James	94
Osborne. Edwin N. Jr.	00	Ray. Thomas DOL '61 Cuba	79
Packard. Ronald L.	97	Reaid. Rollie K.	85
Page. Godon L.	98	Reed. Terry M.	88
Panek. Robert J. Sr.	89	Reid. Harold E.	99
Parker. Frank C. III	00	Reid. Jon E	99
Parker. Maxim Charles	01	Reilly. Edward Daniel Jr.	89
Parker. Woodrow W.	98	Reilly. Lavern G.*	99
Parsons. Don B. Jr.	2	Rex. Robert A.	96
Paschall. Ronald Page	94	Reynolds. E.J. R.	84
Paul. Craig A.	77	Rich. Richard	00
Paulson. Merlyn L.	86	Richardson. Floyd W.	89
Paxton. Donald E.	00	Richtseig. David John	74
Payne. John Allen	73	Rissi. Donald L.	78
Pearce. Edwin Jack*	86	Roach. Marion Lee	73
Pearson. Robert Harvey	88	Roark. Anund C.	79
Pearson. Wayne E.	93	Roark. William Marshall*	77
Pearson. William R.	97	Robbins. Richard Joseph	96
Pemberton. Gene T.	74	Roberts. Gerald Ray	96
Pender. Orland James Jr	96	Robinson. Kenneth D.	88
Perry. Richard Clark#	86	Robinson. Lewis M.	99
Perry. Ronald D.	75	Roby. Charles D.	89
Peters. Charles Henry#	88	Rodriguez. Albert E.	89
Petersen. Gaylord D.	78	Rogers. Kemmeth B.	84
Petrilla. John J.	72	Romano. Gerald Michael	88
Pfeifer. Ronald E.	69	Romine. ALbert W.	79
Pirkle. Lowell Z.	96	Ross. Douglas A.	98
Pitzen. John Russell	96	Ross. Jlvnn Jr.	96
Plants. Thomas Lee	91	Rowley. Charles S.~*	95
Pleiman. James Edward	89	Rudolph. Robert David	88
Pollin. George J.	90	Ruffin. James Thomas	83
Pool. Jerry*	01	Russell. Donald M.	96
Port. William D	95	Salinas. Mercedes Perez	74
Porterfield. Dale K.	72	Salzarulo. Raymond Paul Jr.	91
Potter. William Joseph Jr.	95	Sampson. Leslie Verne	91
Powell. Lynn Kesler	83	Sanderlin. William D.	90
Powell. William E.	85	Sandner. Robert Louis	96
Powers. John L.	01	Sandoval. Antonio R.	00
Powers. Trent Richard	87	Sansone. Dominick (NMN)	84
Poynor. Daniel Roberts	95	Sather. Richard Christian#	85
Prater. Roy D.	97	Schaneberg. Leroy Clyde~	95
Preiss. Robert F.	98	Schimberg. James P.	98
Prescott. Milton E. Jr.	n/a	Schmidt. Norman	74
Preston. James A.*	99	Scholz. Klaus D.	90
Primm. Severo J. III~	96	Schreckengost. Fred T.	91
Pruner. William R.	66	Seagroves. Michael Anthony	74
Pugh. Kenneth W.	75	Seward. William H.	00
Purcell. Howard Philip	96	Shank. Gary Leslie	84
Putnam. Charles Lancaster	88	Shanley. Michael Henry Jr.*	93
Pyles. Harley Boyd	01	Sherburn. Hugh L.	70
Ouamo. George	74	Sherman. John B.	98
Rafael Cruz. Raphael (NMN)~	96	Sherman. Peter W.#	91
Ragsdale. Thomas	69	Sherman. Robert C.	85
Ramsay. Charles J.	01	Shine. Anthony C.	96
Ramsower. Irving B. II	86	Shingledecker. Armon D.	98
Ratzel. Wesley D.	89	Shumway. Geofrey AR.	02
Ravencraft. James Alvin	69	Sijan. Lance P.	74

Sikkink. Roy Dean	69		Trier. Robert D.	82
Simmons. Robert E.*	86		Trimble. Larry Allen	89
Singer. Donald M.	77		Trujillo. Joseph F.	92
Sisson. Winfield Wade	01		Tucker. Edwin Byron	88
Sittner. Ronald N.	97		Tullier. Lonnie J.	68
Slater. Freddie Leon	72		Turley. Morvan D.	67
Sleeman. Christopher J.	84		Turner. Kelton	00
Smith. Edward D. Jr	86		Underwood. Paul G.	98
Smith. Gene Albert	89		Unger. Don Lee	72
Smith. Harold V.	0		Urlinger. Barton J.	68
Smith. Herbert E.	88		Van Buren. Gerald G.	00
Smith. Homer Leroy	74		Van de Geer (or Vandegeer). Richard	00
Smith. Richard D.	94		Van Dyke. Richard Haven	81
Smith. Roger L.	99		Vanden Evkel.Martin D.II~*	90
Smith. William A. Jr.	00		Vanrenselaar. Larry Jack	90
Spencer. Warren R.	77		Varnado. Michael B.	89
Spengler. Henry Mershon III	89		Vennick. Robert N.	01
Spitz. George R.	95		Vescelius. Milton James	85
Sprague. Stanley George	90		Vinson. Bobby G.	98
Squire. Boyd E.	95		Vollmer. Valentine Barnard	74
Stacks. Raymond C.	90		Wade. Barton Scott	85
Stamm. Ernest Albert	74		Wadsworth. Dean A.	99
Stanley. Charles L.	02		Wagener. David R.	97
Stanton. Ronald	01		Wallace. Hobart M.	02
Stearns. Roger Horace	90		Wallace. Michael Walter	89
Stephensen. Mark L.	88		Walsh. Francis A. Jr.	85
Stewart. Donald David	74		Walters. Donovan K.	88
Stinson. William S	99		Walters. Jack	74
Stolz. Lawrence G.	90		Walters. Tim L.	99
Storz. Ronald Edward	74		Walton. Wilbert	92
Stubberfield. Robert A.	89		Wanzel. Charles J. III	86
Sullivan. Farrell Junior	83		Warren. Arthur L.	86
Sullivan. James Edward	85		Waterman. Craig Houston	93
Sullivan. John B. III	90		Waters. Samuel E.	77
Swanson. Jon E.	02		Wax. David J.#	93
Swanson. Kevin C.	84		Weatherby. Jack Wilton	78
Tapp. Marshall L.	99		Wenaas. Gordon J.	00
Taylor. Edd D.	01		Weskamp. Robert L.	74
Taylor. Jesse Junio	75		Wheeler. James Atlee	01
Taylor. Phillip Charles	93		White. Danforth E.	98
Teague. James Erlan	77		Widdis. James W. Jr.	96
Teran. Rufugio T.	02		Widener. Larry Allen	68
Thomas. Harry Eugene	96		Widerquist. Thomas Carl	72
Thomas. Kenneth D. Jr.	85		Wiggins. Wallace L.	78
Thomas. Leo Tarlton Jr.	95		Wilburn. Woodrow Hoover	90
Thomas. Michael W.	84		Wilkins. George H.	96
Thomas. Robert J.	78		Wilkinson. Clyde D.	99
Thompson. George W.	99		Wilkinson. Dennis E.	78
Thompson. Victor Hugo III	73		Williams James E.	99
Thum. Richard Cobb	77		Williams. Billie J.	90
Thurman. Curtis Frank	93		Williams. David B.	89
Todd. William Anthony	86		Williams. David R.	02
Tolbert. Clarence Orfield	89		Williams. Howard K.	92
Toomey. Samuel K. III	90		Williams. James R.	00
Towery. Herman	64		Williams. Richard F.	85
Towle. John C.	95		Williams. Robert C.	95
Townsend. Francis W.	02		Williams. Thaddeus E.	98

Williamson. Don Ira#	89	Wright. Donald L.	95
Wilson. Claude David Jr.	89	Wright. Frederick W.	90
Wilson. Gordon Scott	86	Wright. James J.	78
Wilson. Mickey Allen	99	Wright. Jerdy Albert Jr.	89
Wilson. Robert Allan~	94	Wrye. Blair C.	90
Wilson. Roger E.	88	Wynne. Patrick E.	77
Wimbrow. Nutter J.	77	Yarbrough. William P. Jr.	85
Windeler. Charles Carl Jr.	89	Yonan. Kenneth Joseph	88
Winningham. John O.	85	Young. Robert M.	97
Winston. Charles C. III	77	Zawtocki. Joseph S. Jr.	85
Wolpe. Jack	01	Zook. Harold J.	86
Wonn. James Charles	93	Zukowski. Robert John	96
Worrell. Paul L.	85		

For further clarification:

30 military men escaped

536 military men were repatriated Feb/Mar/Apr 1973 in Operation Homecoming.

95 military men were released to US control before the end of hostilities in 1973.

Men Buried Without Remains

NATIONAL ALLIANCE OF FAMILIES FOR THE RETURN OF AMERICA'S MISSING SERVICEMEN
WORLD WAR II – KOREA - COLD WAR – VIETNAM

BITS 'N' PIECES   FEBRUARY 28, 1998

How widespread is the practice of identifying men without remains?? Here is our short and definitely incomplete list. Please let us know who we missed, and we will publish an updated list in a future edition of "Bits."

Note: this list does not include men with suspect identifications based on a tooth.* Nor does it include men from the "Specter 17" loss whose identifications are highly suspect (in two of those cases the identifications were rescinded.)

Men Buried Without Remains

Thomas Adachi	Gerald Ayers	Donald J. Matejov
William Brooks	Richard M. Cole	Charles S. Rowley
Donald G. Fisher	Stephen Harris	Marshall Tapp
Robert Ireland	Gary LaBohn	Lavern Reilly
Peter R. Matthes	Jacob Mercer	George Thompson
Todd Melton	Richard Nyhof	James Preston
John C. Towle	Robert Wilson	James Williams
Ronnie Hensley	Dale Brandenburg	William Madison Lint
	Charlie B. Davis	

Remains Returned information from:
 Department of Defense, Washington Headquarters Services, Directorate for Information Operations and Reports
DoD Internet website www.dtic.mil/dpmo 07/24/02
National Alliance of Families For The Return Of America's Missing Servicemen World War II – Korea - Cold War – Vietnam
Personal contact with Family Members.

Military Prisoners of War
Released, Repatriated, Escaped

Last Name	First	Middle
Abbott	Joseph	S, Jr.
Abbott	Robert	Archie
Abbott	Wilfred	Keese
Acosta	Hector	Michael
Agnew	Alfred	Howard
Agosto-Santos	Jose	
Aiken	Larry	Delarnard
Albert	Keith	Alexander
Alcorn	Wendell	Reed
Alexander	Fernando	
Allwine	David	Franklin
Alpers	John	Hardesty
Alvarez	Everett	(NMN)
Anderson	Gareth	Laverne
Anderson	Roger	Dale
Anderson	John	Thomas
Anderson	John	Wesley
Andrews	Anthony	Charles
Angus	William	Kerr
Anshus	Richard	Cameron
Anton	Francis	Gene
Anzaldua	Jose	Jesus
Archer	Bruce	Raymond
Arcuri	William	Youl
Astorga	Jose	Manuel
Austin	William	Renwick
Ayres	Timothy	Robert
Bagley	Bobby	Ray
Bailey	James	William
Bailey	Lawrence	Robert
Baird	William	Allen
Baker	David	Earle
Baker	Elmo	Clinnard
Baker	Veto	Huapili
Baldock	Frederick	Charles
Ballard	Arthur	Theodore
Ballenger	Orville	Roger
Barbay	Lawrence	(nmn)
Barnett	Robert	Warren
Barrett	Thomas	Joseph
Barrows	Henry	Charles
Bates	Richard	Lyman
Baugh	William	Joseph
Bean	William	Raymond
Bean	James	Ellis
Bedinger	Henry	James
Beekman	William	David
Beeler	Carroll	Robert
Beens	Lynn	Richard
Bell	James	Franklin
Berg	Kile	Dag
Berger	James	Robert
Bernasconi	Louis	Henry
Biss	Robert	Irvin
Black	Arthur	Neil
Black	Cole	(nmn)
Black	Jon	David
Blevins	John	Charles
Bliss	Ronald	Glenn
Bolstad	Richard	Eugene
Bomar	Jack	Williamson
Borling	John	Lorin
Boyd	Charles	Graham
Boyer	Terry	Lee
Brady	Allen	Colby
Branch	Michael	Patrick
Brande	Harvey	Gordon
Braswell	Donald	Robert
Brazelton	Michael	Lee
Breckner	William	John
Brenneman	Richard	Charles
Brewer	Lee	
Bridger	Barry	Burton
Brigham	James	W
Brodak	John	Warren
Brown	Charles	Arthur
Brown	Paul	Gordon
Browning	Ralph	Thomas
Brudno	Edward	Alan
Brunhaver	Richard	Martin
Brunson	Cecil	H
Brunstrom	Alan	Leslie
Buchanan	Hubert	Elliot
Budd	Leonard	R., Jr.
Burer	Arthur	William
Burgess	Richard	Gordon
Burns	Donald	Ray
Burns	John	Douglass
Burns	Michael	Thomas
Burroughs	William	David
Butcher	Jack	Meyring
Butler	Phillip	Neal
Butler	William	Wallace
Byrne	Ronald	Edward
Byrns	William	Glen

Callaghan	Peter	Alfred
Camacho	Isaac	
Camerota	Peter	Paul
Campbell	Burton	Wayne
Carey	David	Jay
Carlson	Albert	Edwin
Carpenter	Allan	Russell
Carpenter	Joe	Vann
Carrigan	Larry	Edward
Cassell	Harley	M
Cavaiani	Jon	R
Cerak	John	P
Certain	Robert	Glenn
Chambers	Carl	Dennis
Chapman	Harlan	Page
Charles	Norris	Alphonzo
Chauncey	Arvin	Roy
Cheney	Kevin	Joseph
Chenoweth	Robert	Preston
Cherry	Fred	Vann
Chesley	Larry	James
Chevalier	John	R
Chirichigno	Luis	Genardo
Christian	Michael	Durham
Cius	Frank	Edward
Clark	John	Walter
Clements	James	Arlen
Clower	Claude	Douglas
Coffee	Gerald	Leonard
Coker	George	Thomas
Collins	James	Quincy
Collins	Thomas	Edward
Condon	James	C
Conlee	William	W
Cook	James	Raymond
Copeland	H	C
Cordier	Kenneth	William
Cormier	Arthur	
Coskey	Kenneth	Leon
Crafts	Charles	Earle
Craner	Robert	Roger
Crayton	Render	
Crecca	Joseph	
Cronin	Michael	Paul
Crow	Frederick	Austin
Crowe	Winfred	D
Crowson	Frederick	H
Crumpler	Carl	Bovette
Curtis	Thomas	Jerry
Cusimano	Samuel	Bolden
Cutter	James	D
Daigle	Glenn	Henri
Daly	James	Alexander, Jr.
Daniels	Verlyne	Wayne
Daugherty	Lenard	Edward
Daughtrey	Robert	Norlan
Davies	John	Owen

Davis	Edward	Anthony
Davis	Thomas	James
Day	George	Everette
Deering	John	Arthur
DeLuca	Anthony	J
Dengler	Dieter	
Denton	Jeremiah	Andrew
DeSpiegler	Gale	Albert
DiBernado	James	Vincent
Dierling	Edward	A
Dingee	David	Burgoyne
Dodson	James	
Donald	Myron	Lee
Doremus	Robert	Bartsch
Doss	Dale	Walter
Doughty	Daniel	James
Drabic	Peter	E
Dramesi	John	Arthur
Driscoll	Jerry	Donald
Drummond	David	Ian
Duart	David	Henry
Dunn	John	Galbreath
Dunn	John	Howard
Dutton	Richard	Allen
Eastman	Leonard	Corbett
Eckes	Walter	W
Elander	William	J., Jr.
Elbert	Fred	
Elias	Edward	K
Elliott	Artice	W
Ellis	Leon	Francis
Ellis	Jeffrey	Thomas
Ensch	John	C
Estes	Edward	Dale
Ettmueller	Harry	L
Everett	David	A.
Everson	David	
Fann	Jerry	L
Fant	Robert	StClair
Fellowes	John	Heaphy
Fer	John	
Finlay	John	Stewart
Fisher	Kenneth	
Fisher	John	B
Fleenor	Kenneth	Raymond
Flesher	Hubert	Kelly
Flom	Fredric	Russell
Flora	Carroll	E
Flynn	John	Peter
Flynn	Robert	James
Forby	Willis	Ellis
Ford	David	Edward
Fowler	Henry	Pope
Francis	Richard	L
Frank	Martin	S
Franke	Fred	Augustus
Fraser	Kenneth	J

Friese	Lawrence	Victor
Frishmann	Robert	F
Fryett	George	F
Fuller	Robert	Byron
Fulton	Richard	J
Gaddis	Norman	Carl
Gaither	Ralph	Ellis
Galanti	Paul	Edward
Galati	Ralph	William
Gartley	Markham	Ligon
Gauntt	William	Aaron
Geloneck	Terry	M
Gerndt	Gerald	Lee
Gideon	Willard	Selleck
Gillespie	Charles	R
Giroux	Peter	J
Glenn	Danny	Elloy
Glenn	Thomas	Paul
Goodermote	Wayne	Keith
Gostas	Theodore	W
Gotner	Norbert	A
Gough	James	W
Gouin	Donat	Joseph
Graening	Bruce	A
Granger	Paul	L
Grant	David	B
Gray	David	Fletcher
Greene	Charles	E
Gregory	Kenneth	R
Grigsby	Donald	E
Groom	George	Edward
Gruters	Guy	Dennis
Guarino	Lawrence	Nicholas
Guenther	Lynn	E
Guffey	Jerry	
Guggenberger	Gary	John
Gurnsey	Earl	F
Guttersen	Laird	
Guy	Theodore	Wilson
Haines	Collins	Henry
Hall	Thomas	Renwick
Hall	Keith	Norman
Hall	George	Robert
Halyburton	Porter	Alex
Hamilton	Walter	D
Hanson	Gregg	O
Hanton	Thomas	J
Hardman	William	Morgan
Hardy	William	H
Harker	David	Northrup
Harris	Carlyle	Smith
Harris	Jessie	B
Hatch	Paul	G
Hatcher	David	Burnett
Hawley	Edwin	A., Jr.
Hayhurst	Robert	A
Heeren	Jerome	D

Hefel	Daniel	
Hegdahl	Douglas	B
Heilig	John	
Heiliger	Donald	Lester
Helle	Robert	R
Henderson	William	J
Henry	Nathan	Barney
Henry	Lee	Edward
Herlik	Querin	E
Hess	Jay	Criddle
Hestand	James	Hardy
Hickerson	James	Martin
Higdon	Kenneth	W
Hildebrand	Leland	Louis
Hill	Howard	John
Hinckley	Robert	Bruce
Hiteshew	James	Edward
Hivner	James	Otis
Hoffman	David	Wesley
Hoffson	Arthur	Thomas
Horinek	Ramon	Anton
Horio	Thomas	Teruo
Hubbard	Edward	Lee
Hudson	Robert	M
Hughes	James	Lindberg
Hughey	Kenneth	Raymond
Hunsucker	James	
Hutton	James	Leo
Hyatt	Leo	Gregory
Ingvalson	Roger	Dean
Iodice	Frank	C
Jackson	James	E
Jackson	Charles	A
Jacquez	Juan	L
James	Gobel	Dale
James	Charlie	Negus
Jayroe	Julius	Skinner
Jefcoat	Carl	H
Jeffrey	Robert	Duncan
Jenkins	Harry	Tarleton
Jensen	Jay	Robert
Johnson	Samuel	Robert
Johnson	Harold	E
Johnson	Kenneth	Richard
Johnson	Edward	Robert
Johnson	Bobby	Louis
Johnson	Richard	E
Jones	Murphy	Neal
Jones	Robert	Campbell
Jones	Thomas	N
Kari	Paul	Anthony
Kasler	James	Helms
Kavanaugh	Abel	L
Keirn	Richard	Paul
Kernan	Joseph	Eugene
Kerns	Gail	M
Kerr	Michael	Scott

Kev	Wilson	Denver
Kientzler	Phillip	Allan
King	Everett	Melborne, Jr.
Kirk	Thomas	Henry
Kittinger	Joseph	W., Jr.
Klomann	Thomas	J
Klusmann	Charles	F
Knutson	Rodney	Allen
Kobashigawa	Tom	Y
Kopfman	Theodore	Frank
Kramer	Galand	Dwight
Kramer	Terry	L
Kroboth	Alan	J
Kula	James	D
Kushner	Floyd	Harold
LaBeau	Michael	H
Lamar	James	Lasley
Lane	Michael	Christopher
Larson	Gordon	Albert
Lasiter	Carl	William
Latella	George	F
Latendresse	Thomas	Bennett
Latham	James	Downs
Lawrence	William	Porter
Lebert	Ronald	Merl
LeBlanc	Louis	E., Jr.
Lehnrn	Gary	Robert
Lehrman	Ronald	John
Lengvel	Lauren	Robert
Lenker	Michael	Robert
Leonard	Edward	W
Leopold	Stephen	Ryder
Lerseth	Roger	G
Lesesne	Henry	D
Lewis	Frank	D
Lewis	Earl	Gardner
Lewis	Robert	
Lewis	Keith	H
Ligon	Vernon	Peyton
Lilly	Warren	Robert
Lockhart	Hayden	James
Logan	Donald	K
Lollar	James	L
Long	Stephen	G
Long	Julius	Wollen, Jr.
Low	James	Frederick
Luna	Jose	David
Lurie	Alan	Pierce
MacPhail	Don	Alan
Madden	Roy, Jr.	
Madison	Thomas	Mark
Makowski	Louis	Frank
Malo	Isaako	Fa'atoese
Marshall	Marion	A
Martin	Edward	Holmes
Martin	Donald	Eugene
Martini	Michael	R
Marvel	Jerry	Wendell
Maslowski	Daniel	F
Masterson	Frederick	J
Mastin	Ronald	Lambert
Matagulay	Roque	S
Matheny	David	P
Matsui	Melvin	K
Mayall	William	T
Mayhew	William	John
McCain	John	Sidney
McClure	Claude	D
McCuistion	Michael	K
McCullough	Ralph	W
McDaniel	Norman	Alexander
McDaniel	Eugene	Baker
McDow	Richard	H
McGrath	John	Michael
McKamey	John	Bryan
McKnight	George	Grigsby
McManus	Kevin	Joseph
McMillan	Isiah	R
McMorrow	John	P
McMurray	Frederick	C
McMurray	William	G
McMurray	Cordine	
McNish	Thomas	Mitchell
McSwain	George	Palmer
Means	William	Harley
Mechenbier	Edward	John
Mecleary	Read	Blaine
Mehl	James	Patrick
Mehrer	Gustav	Alois
Merritt	Raymond	James
Metzger	William	John
Meyer	Alton	Benno
Miller	Roger	Alan
Miller	Edison	Wainright
Miller	Edwin	Frank
Milligan	Joseph	Edward
Mobley	Joseph	Scott
Moe	Thomas	Nelson
Molinare	Albert	R
Monlux	Harold	Deloss
Montague	Paul	Joseph
Moore	Dennis	Anthony
Moore	Ernest	Milvin
Morgan	Herschel	Scott
Morgan	Gary	L
Mott	David	P
Mullen	Richard	Dean
Mulligan	James	Alfred
Murphy	John	S., Jr.
Myers	Armand	Jesse
Myers	Glenn	Leo
Nagahiro	James	Y
Nakagawa	Gordon	R
Nasmyth	John	Herbert

Naughton	Robert	John
Neco-Quinones	Felix	
Nelson	Steven	N
Neuens	Martin	James
Newcomb	Wallace	Grant
Newell	Stanley	Arthur
Nichols	Aubrey	Allen
Nix	Cowan	Glenn
Norrington	Giles	Roderick
Norris	Thomas	Elmer
North	Joseph	S., Jr.
North	Kenneth	Walter
Nowicki	James	Ernest
O'Connor	Michael	Francis
Odell	Donald	Eugene
O'Neil	James	W
Ortiz-Rivera	Luis	A
Osborne	Dale	Harrison
Osburn	Laird	P
Overly	Norris	M
Padgett	James	P
Page	Jasper	Nelba
Paige	Gordon	Curtis
Parrott	Thomas	Vance
Parsels	John	William
Peel	Robert	D
Penn	Michael	Gene
Perkins	Glendon	William
Perricone	Richard	Robert
Peterson	Douglas	Brian
Peterson	Michael	T
Pfister	James	F., Jr.
Pirie	James	Glenn
Pitchford	John	Joseph
Pitzer	Daniel	L
Plumb	Joseph	Charles
Polfer	Clarence	Ronald
Pollack	Melvin	(nmn)
Pollard	Ben	M
Potter	Albert	J
Prather	Phillip	Dean
Price	Donald	E
Price	Larry	D
Profilet	Leo	Twyman
Pryor	Robert	J
Purcell	Benjamin	H
Purcell	Robert	Baldwin
Purrington	Frederick	Raym
Pyle	Thomas	Shaw
Pyle	Darrel	Edwin
Quinn	Francis	
Raebel	Dale	V
Randall	Robert	I
Rander	Donald	J
Ratzlaff	Brian	M
Ratzlaff	Richard	Raymond
Ray	Johnnie	L

Ray	James	Edwin
Rayford	King	David, Jr.
Reeder	William	S
Rehmann	David	George
Reich	William	John
Reynolds	Jon	Anzuena
Riate	Alfonso	Ray
Rice	Charles	Donald
Ridgeway	Ronald	Lewis
Riess	Charles	F
Ringsdorf	Herbert	Benjamin
Risner	Robinson	
Risner	Richard	F
Rivers	Wendell	Burke
Robinson	Paul	K
Robinson	William	Andrew
Rodriquez	Ferdinand	A
Roha	Michael	R
Rollins	David	John
Rose	Joseph	
Rose	George	A
Rowe	James	Nicholas
Rudloff	Stephen	A
Ruhling	Mark	John
Rumble	Wesley	L
Runyan	Albert	Edward
Russell	Kay	
Rutledge	Howard	Elmer
Sandvick	Robert	James
Sawhill	Robert	Ralston
Schierman	Wesley	Duane
Schoeffel	Peter	VanRuyter
Schrump	Raymond	Cecil
Schulz	Paul	Henry
Schweitzer	Robert	James
Schwertfeger	William	R
Seeber	Bruce	G
Seek	Brian	J
Sehorn	James	Eldon
Sexton	John	C
Shanahan	Joseph	Francis
Shankel	William	Leonard
Shattuck	Lewis	Wiley
Shepard	Vernon	C
Shingaki	Tomatsu	
Shively	James	Richard
Shore	Edward	R., Jr.
Shumaker	Robert	Harper
Shuman	Edwin	Arthur
Sienicki	Theodore	S
Sigler	Gary	Richard
Sima	Thomas	W
Simms	Harold	D
Simonet	Kenneth	Adrian
Simpson	Richard	T
Singleton	Jerry	Allen
Smith	George	Edward

Phonies, Website

If the name you are looking for is not on the previous lists, the name you are checking does NOT belong to a POW or MIA, returnee, releasee or escapee. Please see our website, **www.pownetwork.org**, click PHONIES.

The questionable claims can be further substantiated as legitimate or not by the DPMO Public Affairs Office, 703-602-2102, extension 169.

Data Source: Defense Prisoner of War/Missing Personnel Office Reference Document.... U.S. Personnel Missing, Southeast Asia (and Selected Foreign Nationals) {PMSEA} dated May 2001 DPMO/RD.

Contacts

P.O.W. NETWORK
Box 68
Skidmore, MO 64487- 0068

Phone - 660-928-3304
FAX - 660-928-3303

Website: http://www.pownetwork.org
email: info@pownetwork.org

The P.O.W. NETWORK is an educational not-for-profit 501 (c)(3) organization. Donations are tax-deductible per IRS regulations. The NETWORK receives NO Government or private grants. The historical preservation project is funded by donations from the public. The website is managed by P.O.W. NETWORK Chairman, Chuck Schantag and his wife, Mary.

For writing letters to a returnee: Please stamp, seal and address your envelope with NAME ONLY. Mail that in another envelope to the NETWORK address. We forward the same day mail is received.

For LOVELETTERS to the family of a POW/MIA/KIA: Letters will be posted to the Internet site as they are received. We CANNOT forward – we do NOT have family addresses. If you do not have email, be sure to include a postal address for families to respond. Mail to the above NETWORK address.

Permission Acknowledgements

Every effort was made to ensure that required permissions to reprint all materials were obtained prior to publication. With the transient nature of our society, the email address for many was no longer valid. We are grateful for the permissions received to reprint the LOVELETTERS previously posted publicly at www.pownetwork.org. The letters have been reproduced, with only minor edits, as we have received them since 1998.

Permission granted to reproduce LOVELETTERS:

Amicalement, Yvan Leriche	August 20, 2002 by email
Arfmann, Donna	July 10, 2002 by email
Backhurst, Ann	July 8, 2002 by email
Bailey, Lisa	July 8, 2002 by email
Butler, Karene	July 8, 2002 by email
Carpenter, Al	July 8, 2002 by email
Chandler, Chick	July 8, 2002 by email
Garcia, Laura	July 9, 2002 by email
Gisin, Marilynne	July 8, 2002 by email
Herron, Janet	July 9, 2002 by email
Hivner, James Otis	July 13, 2002 by email
Horning, William	August 3, 2002 by email
Johns, Robert Jr.	July 8, 2002 by email
Layne, Barbara	July 8, 2002 by email
McDonald, Judyth M	July 9, 2002 by email
McGinnis, Jim	August 5, 2002 by email
Morgan, Col. Scotty	July 9, 2002 by phone
Nemnich, Debi,	July20, 2002 by email
Owings, Karen	July 9, 2002 by email
Philip, Davis	July 8, 2002 by email
Pusieski, John	July 28, 2002 by email
Rehl, Mark A.	July 8, 2002 by email
Stirling-Stevens, Diane	July 8, 2002 by email
Teleha, Thomas M.HM1(SS/FMF) USN	July 11, 2002 by email
Turk, Gary S.	July 8, 2002 by email
Weckstein, Laurie	July 21, 2002 by email
Welsch, Jane	July 8, 2002 by email

Photo Credits, Identifications

The photos reproduced in *More Than A Band Of Metal* capture just a small part of a monumental time in our history. Since 1998, we have attempted to identify those returning P.O.W.s depicted in these United States Air Force photos. It is an ongoing project. Where identification has been made, it is noted below.*

The photos were originally taken by United Sates Air Force photographers at several various bases during Homecoming (Feb-April 1973). Museum Curator, Lee Humiston, shared the photos with us. Ranks below are RETIREMENT rank.

Page 2, Hoa Lo Prison, nicknamed the Hanoi Hilton by American pilots held captive there.
Page 6, unknown
Page 8, In front, Zuhoski, Cmd. Charles P. USN (Ret) and Copeland, Col. H.C., USAF (Ret) 03/14/73 (USAF photo by Tsgt Robert N. Denham)
Page 11, Gia Lam airfield near Hanoi.
Page 17, Moore, Thomas – POW/DIC/PFOD, top; Shelton Charles – POW/PFOD, bottom left; Humphrey, Galen – KIA/BNR, bottom right. All photos provided by families.
Page 19, unknown
Page 20, unknown
Page 23, Hess, LtCol Jay, USAF (Ret)
Page 25, unknown
Page 26, unknown
Page 29, Terwilliger, Virgil – KIA/BNR, top left; Pool, Jerry Lynn – MIA/PFOD, group remains I.D. disputed by family, top right; Gourley, Laurent, MIA/PFOD, bottom. All photos provided by families.
Page 33, Davis, Capt. Edward USN (Ret) and Ma-Co.
Page 35, unknown
Page 39, Thompson, Col. Floyd USA, (Ret), longest held POW, deceased.
Page 42, Parsels, Maj. John USA (Ret)
Page 47, Springman, Richard E4 USA
Page 51, Fer, Col. John USAF (Ret) and mom
Page 53 and 69, Baker, B/Gen David USAF (Ret), 02/12/73, Loc Ninh RVN.
Page 57, unknown

Page 59, Cronin, Capt. Michael J. USNR (Ret) (USAF Photo by SSgt Larry Wright).

Page 61, unknown

Page 63, Seek, Col. Brian USAF (Ret)

Page 65, unknown

Page 67, unknown

Page 71, Mullens, Capt. Richard "Moon" USN (Ret) and his bracelet wearer, Debra Davis Howard at Clark Air Force Base. *NOTE: Moon and Debra have maintained contact. She is now happily married, with 3 boys of her own. Her father was an Air Force Captain at the time.*

Page 76, Adkins, Maj. Clodean USA (Ret) CIV deceased

Page 83, Flynn, LtGen. John Peter USAF (Ret), deceased.

Page 85, Peterson, Ambassador Douglas "Pete" and Carlotta

Page 89, unknown

Page 94, unknown

Page 95, Right to Left: Kobashigawa, Tom; Parsels, Maj John USA (Ret); Tabb, MSgt Robert USA (Ret); Elliot, Col Artice USA (Ret); Alwine, Msgt. David USA (Ret); Anshus, Lt Col Richard USA (Ret); Malo, Issako; Prather, CW4 Phillip USA (Ret); Lenker, Michael; Caviani, SGM Jon USA (Ret); Mott, Col David USAF (Ret)

Page 99, Rice, Cmdr. Charles, USN (Ret)

Page 102, unknown

Page 107, unknown

Page 109, White, Maj. Robert, USA (Ret).

Page 115, Drabik, Peter; Long, Julius Jr.; Baird, William; Kerns, Gail. Photo provided by Joe Waskas.

Page 117, Maddden, SSgt Roy Jr USAF (Ret), deceased.

Page 121, Ragland, Dayton – MIA/PFOD, POW Returnee Korea, top left; Handrahan, Eugene – MIA/PFOD, top right; Milliner, Patrick –MIA/PFOD, bottom left; Rowe, James "Nick" (escapee/assassinated). All photos provided by families.

Page 123, unknown

Page 125, Jensen, LtCol Jay USAF (Ret), deceased.

Page 127, Hivner, Col. James, USAF (Ret); USAF Freedom Flight 191, Photo courtesy Col. Hivner.

* Our thanks to Lee Humiston, Col Dave Ford USAF (Ret), Dennis Chambers, Lt Col John Dunn USA (Ret), Col Bill Reeder Jr, USA (Ret), CW4 Roy Ziegler USA (Ret), Col Jim Lamar USAF (Ret), Capt Leo Profilet, USN (Ret), Maj Dick Vaughn USAF (Ret), Cdr JB Souder, USN (Ret), Cdr Al Carpenter USN (Ret), MSgt Joe Waskas USA SF (Ret) for help in identifying the returnees in the photos.

Index

Order Blank

P.O.W. NETWORK
Box 68
Skidmore, MO 64487-0068
660-928-3304 for phone orders

DARE TO CARE!!

P.O.W. Bracelets
Aluminum _____ @ $7.00 each   Stainless Steel _____@ $8.00 each
Vietnam _____ Gulf War, Michael Speicher _____ Other_____ (attach details)
ANY name   Army _____ Navy_____ Air Force_____ Marine Corps _____

P.O.W. Flag, double sided, outdoor 3' x 5', _____@ 32.00 each   _____
P.O.W. Window Decals, _____ at 3 for $1.00   _____
Additional Copies of ***More than a Band of Metal***, _____@ $17.95 _____

All prices include shipping and handling.   **Total** _____

Ship to:
Name:_____
Address: _____
City: _____ **State:** _____ **Zip:** _____

Visa ____ **MC** ____ **Discover**_____ **Expiration Date** _____
Credit Card Number _____
Signature_____
Phone number or email: _____

Makes checks payable P.O.W. NETWORK
Allow 6-8 weeks for delivery

—